BOOT CAMP FOR LEAP 2025

BETTER SCORES IN ONE DAY

Subject: **U.S. HISTORY**

Stephanie Constantino

Inquiries concerning this publication should be mailed to:
MasteryPrep
7117 Florida Blvd.
Baton Rouge, LA 70806

MasteryPrep is a trade name and/or trademark of MasteryPrep, LLC.
This publication, its author, and its publisher are in no way affiliated with or authorized by the Louisiana Department of Education. LEAP 2025® is a registered trademark of the Louisiana Department of Education.

ISBN: 978-1-960663-01-6

A LETTER TO STUDENTS

To the LEAP 2025 student heading into test day,

I want to start by saying that we get it. We know the pressure on your shoulders as test day looms in your near future. There's a lot riding on that score. Schools will use that number to make a lot of big decisions about your future. And to relieve that pressure, I want to offer two things:

Number 1: It's a standardized test. It's made up of multiple-choice questions, trap answers, and the fact that it doesn't give us a clear picture of who you are as a person. Those scores can't show whether you'll be an amazing business owner or a professional athlete. They can't show school administrators just how artistically talented you are or whether your musical abilities are guaranteed to take you to #1 on the charts. And they don't show how kind, hardworking, and determined you are.

While these scores might give a little insight into how well you can answer questions, they don't show everything. You are capable and worthy of a happy, successful life, no matter how many questions you get right.

Number 2: We're here to help. We've gathered the most important content, collected the top-tested skills, and zoned in on the kinds of traps you'll run into on test day. And the result of all this? The Boot Camp for LEAP 2025 U.S. History. In this workshop, you'll learn strategies and practice using tools that are guaranteed to raise your score.

We know it's a lot to ask, but if you stick with us for the next few hours and work hard alongside your instructor, you'll walk into class on test day with everything you need to hit that goal score.

We wish you all the luck on test day! (Not that you'll need it, of course.) You've got this.

Cheers,
All of us at MasteryPrep

CONTENTS

ITEM SET WALKTHROUGH 85

MINI-TEST 99

CONCLUSION 111

CONTRIBUTORS 115

SECTION 1
ORIENTATION

Why Does This Test Matter?

Instructions

Refer to the information below as your instructor leads the discussion.

The LEAP 2025 U.S. History test is what's known as an EOC (End of Course) Exam. Why does it matter to you?

- Avoid summer school

- Graduate

- Improve college readiness

- Boost your final history grade

To graduate from high school, you need to pass this test. What opportunities does a high school diploma create?

- About 40% more income

- A 33% greater chance of being hired

- College acceptance

How will passing the LEAP 2025 U.S. History test benefit YOU?

How Is the LEAP 2025 U.S. History Test Scored?

Instructions

Refer to the information below as your instructor leads the discussion.

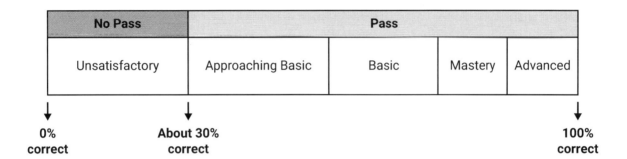

No Pass	Pass			
Unsatisfactory	Approaching Basic	Basic	Mastery	Advanced

↓ **0%** correct   ↓ **About 30%** correct   ↓ **100%** correct

Quick Stats:

- A combination of 50 questions and 1 writing prompt worth 69 total points
  - Questions worth 1–2 points each
  - 1 essay worth 8 points
- About 30% of the available points correct needed to pass
- 225 minutes to finish all 3 sections

1

Since there are 69 points possible, and you need about 30% to pass, how many points do you need to pass?

_____

2

How many points does that mean you can miss?

_____

Note: The percentages on this page are based on historical test score data published by the Louisiana Department of Education.

The LEAP 2025 Sessions

Instructions

Refer to the information below as your instructor leads the discussion. Circle the correct answers.

LEAP 2025 U.S. History by Session

	What's Included?	Points Possible	Time Limit
Session 1	Item Sets + Individual Questions	32–33	80 min
Session 2	Item Set + Task Set	17–18	65 min
Session 3	Item Sets + Individual Questions + Field Test Questions	19	80 min

3

Which session contains the essay prompt?

1 2 3

4

Which session contains the most item sets?

1 2 3

5

Which session will allow you to move at the slowest pace?

1 2 3

Tools of the Trade

Instructions

Place a check mark next to each tool you think you'll have access to on the LEAP 2025 U.S. History test.

☐   Answer cross-off

☐   Flag Question

☐   Highlighter

☐   Sticky Note

☐   Options > Change test color

☐   Line Guide

☐   Masking (hide portions of the test)

☐   Magnifier

What Is a Boot Camp?

Instructions

Refer to the information below as your instructor leads the discussion.

6

Will this Boot Camp be the only thing you use to prepare for the LEAP 2025 U.S. History test? Circle your answer.

Yes   No

7

Place a check mark next to each of the things you should expect from today's Boot Camp.

☐ A variety of test-taking strategies

☐ The most important content that shows up on the test

☐ Everything you could possibly need to know about U.S. history

☐ Examples of questions you can expect to see on the test

☐ How to hack the test and get a perfect score

THE STANDALONES

The Standalones Preview

Instructions

Complete the quiz. If time remains, check your answers.

Question 1

Use the excerpt and what you know about U.S. history to answer the question below.

Excerpt from an Interview with Two Kansans (2003)

This excerpt is from an interview with two women who lived in Kansas during the Great Depression.

Dorothy Hallet: Out of nowhere it came out. It wasn't light, like sand. We saw it, like a black cloud. Did you?

Hattie Baker: Yes. The dogs were barking and the animals went in before it came. Then it was dark. You could barely see down to your toes.

Dorothy Hallet: My parents were . . . trying to wrangle the cows . . . he was looking through the barn where the wind was howling . . . It was so black . . .

Which statement **best** explains how the Dust Bowl contributed to the Great Depression?

A. The reduction in arable land in the Great Plains resulted in the cost of agricultural products rising.

B. The elimination of crops in the Great Plains led to farms being reclaimed by the banks.

C. The wave of farmers selling their land contributed to the stock market crash.

D. The reduction of topsoil in the Great Plains led to people migrating to industrial centers in the Northeast.

Question 2

Use the excerpt and what you know about U.S. history to answer the question below.

Excerpt from *Reaching Adulthood in Mississippi* (1968)

by Sarah Booker

This excerpt by Sarah Booker, an African American student at Rust College in Mississippi and an SNCC volunteer, discusses involvement in the civil rights movement.

[W]e would have day-long petition signings, and at night, we would hold protests. But they were usually small. Many feared being seen. When we started, some wouldn't even speak with our group . . . There were even some [who] didn't know they could vote . . .

As we continued to meet through summer, people started attending. I think they realized our motives were good. But some started getting laid off from work, thrown out of sharecropping, and left on the street . . . SNCC began assigning representatives to college campuses in the North. They went asking for money, food, and clothes for the needy in Mississippi, and the money, food, and clothes started pouring in. The Delta Negroes . . . knew they had found family; family they could rely on . . .

Which statements **best** describe how SNCC helped in the movement to secure civil rights for African Americans? Select **two** correct answers.

A. SNCC appealed to the president to send in federal protection for African Americans.

B. SNCC advocated for African Americans to unite and take action for equality.

C. SNCC representatives spoke out against white supremacists at state colleges and universities.

D. SNCC organized armed resistance in African American towns and cities.

E. SNCC put together voter registration drives in African American towns and cities.

F. SNCC argued against discriminatory practices in Supreme Court cases.

Question 3

Use the excerpt and what you know about U.S. history to answer the question below.

This excerpt is by Private Walter Edwards, an American soldier of the 128th Infantry during World War I. It describes his experience in the trenches.

Excerpt from *In the Trench* (1918)

by Walter Edwards

There was a new kid manning lookout, on this particular morning; I was sitting against the entry, preparing my rounds, when gas shells started raining down.

I didn't hesitate, reaching for my gun immediately, but I was hit on the head and my helmet was dented. My head would have been cracked open if not for my helmet.

My eyes were watering and I lost my breathing for a period, and if it hadn't been for my compatriot next to me, I probably wouldn't be writing this . . .

Which statement **best** describes the effects of gas attacks on the battlefield during World War I?

A. Gas attacks gave Germany a significant advantage and allowed them to overcome Great Britain before the United States entered the conflict.

B. Gas attacks were responsible for millions of casualties and resulted in mass demonstrations against the war.

C. Gas attacks made trench warfare harsh and had a significant psychological impact on soldiers.

D. Gas attacks horrified soldiers and resulted in them demanding a cease-fire to end the war.

Question 4

Use the news article and what you know about U.S. history to answer the question below.

The Oregonian Front Page (March 1, 1917)

Which statement **best** explains how the interception of the Zimmerman Telegram contributed to the eventual entry of the United States into World War I?

A. The revelation of Germany's plans against the United States led many citizens to support joining the war.

B. The information uncovered in the telegram led the United States to create a secret arms pact with Great Britain.

C. The revelation of plans to interfere with United States trade led corporations to support the war effort.

D. The loss of Mexico as an ally led the United States to invade German colonies in South America.

Just the Facts?

Instructions

Refer to the questions below as your instructor leads the discussion. Do not answer the questions.

Option 1

Which of the following quotations appears in the Declaration of Independence?

A. "We the People of the United States, in Order to form a more perfect Union, establish Justice, ensure domestic Tranquility, provide for the common defense, promote the general Welfare, and secure the Blessings of Liberty to ourselves and our Posterity, do ordain and establish this Constitution for the United States of America."

B. "Congress shall make no law respecting an establishment of religion, or prohibiting the free exercise thereof; or abridging the freedom of speech, or of the press; or the right of the people peaceably to assemble, and to petition the Government for a redress of grievances."

C. "We hold these truths to be self-evident, that all men are created equal, that they are endowed by the Creator with certain unalienable Rights, that among these are Life, Liberty, and the pursuit of Happiness."

D. "They who can give up essential liberty to obtain a little temporary safety deserve neither liberty nor safety."

Option 2

Use the excerpt and what you know about U.S. history to answer the question below.

Excerpt from an Interview with Two Kansans (2003)

This excerpt is from an interview with two women who lived in Kansas during the Great Depression.

Dorothy Hallet: Out of nowhere it came out. It wasn't light, like sand. We saw it, like a black cloud. Did you?

Hattie Baker: Yes. The dogs were barking and the animals went in before it came. Then it was dark. You could barely see down to your toes.

Dorothy Hallet: My parents were . . . trying to wrangle the cows . . . he was looking through the barn where the wind was howling . . . It was so black . . .

Which statement **best** explains how the Dust Bowl contributed to the Great Depression?

A. The reduction in arable land in the Great Plains resulted in the cost of agricultural products rising.

B. The elimination of crops in the Great Plains led to farms being reclaimed by the banks.

C. The wave of farmers selling their land contributed to the stock market crash.

D. The reduction of topsoil in the Great Plains led to people migrating to industrial centers in the Northeast.

The Process of Elimination

Instructions

Refer to the question below as your instructor leads the discussion. Circle the correct answer.

The P.O.E.

There are more wrong answers than there are right ones. Instead of searching for the exact right answer, focus on narrowing your options by eliminating the answers you *know* are wrong. If all goes as planned, you'll be left with just one answer: the right one.

Question 1

Use the excerpt and what you know about U.S. history to answer the question below.

Excerpt from an Interview with Two Kansans (2003)

This excerpt is from an interview with two women who lived in Kansas during the Great Depression.

Dorothy Hallet: Out of nowhere it came out. It wasn't light, like sand. We saw it, like a black cloud. Did you?

Hattie Baker: Yes. The dogs were barking and the animals went in before it came. Then it was dark. You could barely see down to your toes.

Dorothy Hallet: My parents were . . . trying to wrangle the cows . . . he was looking through the barn where the wind was howling . . . It was so black . . .

Which statement **best** explains how the Dust Bowl contributed to the Great Depression?

A. The reduction in arable land in the Great Plains resulted in the cost of agricultural products rising.

B. The elimination of crops in the Great Plains led to farms being reclaimed by the banks.

C. The wave of farmers selling their land contributed to the stock market crash.

D. The reduction of topsoil in the Great Plains led to people migrating to industrial centers in the Northeast.

This page intentionally left blank. Content resumes on the next page.

A Little Over-the-Top

Instructions

Refer to the question below as your instructor leads the discussion. Circle two correct answers.

Dramatic Answer Choices

When you're given a passage, some trap answers will go a little too far with the details. They become exaggerations, rather than accurate descriptions of what happened.

Question 2

Use the excerpt and what you know about U.S. history to answer the question below.

Excerpt from *Reaching Adulthood in Mississippi* (1968)

by Sarah Booker

This excerpt by Sarah Booker, an African American student at Rust College in Mississippi and an SNCC volunteer, discusses involvement in the civil rights movement.

[W]e would have day-long petition signings, and at night, we would hold protests. But they were usually small. Many feared being seen. When we started, some wouldn't even speak with our group . . . There were even some [who] didn't know they could vote . . .

As we continued to meet through summer, people started attending. I think they realized our motives were good. But some started getting laid off from work, thrown out of sharecropping, and left on the street . . . SNCC began assigning representatives to college campuses in the North. They went asking for money, food, and clothes for the needy in Mississippi, and the money, food, and clothes started pouring in. The Delta Negroes . . . knew they had found family; family they could rely on . . .

Which statements **best** describe how SNCC helped in the movement to secure civil rights for African Americans? Select **two** correct answers.

A. SNCC appealed to the president to send in federal protection for African Americans.

B. SNCC advocated for African Americans to unite and take action for equality.

C. SNCC representatives spoke out against white supremacists at state colleges and universities.

D. SNCC organized armed resistance in African American towns and cities.

E. SNCC put together voter registration drives in African American towns and cities.

F. SNCC argued against discriminatory practices in Supreme Court cases.

Valuable Resources

Instructions

Refer to the question below as your instructor leads the discussion. Circle the correct answer.

Use Your Sources

At first glance, some resources may seem like they have no connection to the question. But if you're given a source, use it. Eliminate answer choices that don't align with what the source says.

Question 3

Use the excerpt and what you know about U.S. history to answer the question below.

This excerpt is by Private Walter Edwards, an American soldier of the 128th Infantry during World War I. It describes his experience in the trenches.

Excerpt from *In the Trench* (1918)

by Walter Edwards

There was a new kid manning lookout, on this particular morning; I was sitting against the entry, preparing my rounds, when gas shells started raining down.

I didn't hesitate, reaching for my gun immediately, but I was hit on the head and my helmet was dented. My head would have been cracked open if not for my helmet.

My eyes were watering and I lost my breathing for a period, and if it hadn't been for my compatriot next to me, I probably wouldn't be writing this . . .

Which statement **best** describes the effects of gas attacks on the battlefield during World War I?

A. Gas attacks gave Germany a significant advantage and allowed them to overcome Great Britain before the United States entered the conflict.

B. Gas attacks were responsible for millions of casualties and resulted in mass demonstrations against the war.

C. Gas attacks made trench warfare harsh and had a significant psychological impact on soldiers.

D. Gas attacks horrified soldiers and resulted in them demanding a cease-fire to end the war.

Throwing You Off the Scent

Instructions

Refer to the question below as your instructor leads the discussion. Circle the correct answer.

Outliers

Occasionally, answer choices will contain traps that have information that seems to come out of nowhere. Don't let this throw you off your game. Focus on the source and use the process of elimination.

Question 4

Use the news article and what you know about U.S. history to answer the question below.

The Oregonian Front Page (March 1, 1917)

Which statement **best** explains how the interception of the Zimmerman Telegram contributed to the eventual entry of the United States into World War I?

A. The revelation of Germany's plans against the United States led many citizens to support joining the war.

B. The information uncovered in the telegram led the United States to create a secret arms pact with Great Britain.

C. The revelation of plans to interfere with United States trade led corporations to support the war effort.

D. The loss of Mexico as an ally led the United States to invade German colonies in South America.

Test Run

Instructions

Complete the quiz. If time remains, check your answers.

Question 5

Use the excerpt and what you know about U.S. history to answer the question below.

Excerpt from "An Address to the Nation on Vietnam" (May 14, 1969)

by President Richard Nixon

This excerpt is from a 1969 speech given by President Richard Nixon on the United States exit from the Vietnam War.

In determining what choices would be acceptable, we have to understand our essential objective in Vietnam: what we want is very little, but very fundamental. We seek the opportunity for the South Vietnamese people to determine their own political future without outside interference . . .

Let me put it plainly: What the United States wants for South Vietnam is not the important thing. What North Vietnam wants for South Vietnam is not the important thing. What is important is what the people of South Vietnam want for South Vietnam . . .

Which statement **best** explains how President Nixon contributed to the withdrawal of U.S. troops from Vietnam?

A. He supported rebels in overthrowing the government of South Vietnam.

B. He argued that an increase in military spending was necessary to challenge North Vietnam.

C. He moved to withdraw American troops and hand off military responsibilities to South Vietnamese forces.

D. He announced a series of economic actions to assist South Vietnam in the war effort.

Question 6

Use the photograph and what you know about U.S. history to answer the question.

Mechanical Steam Shovel Digging at a PWA (Public Works Administration) Construction Site

Source: Franklin D. Roosevelt Presidential Library and Museum

Which statement **best** details the goal of New Deal agencies and programs such as the Public Works Administration (PWA) in the 1930s?

A. The agencies were created to help the country prepare for a potential war in Europe.

B. The agencies were created to provide opportunities for people to work and improve the American economy.

C. The agencies were established to decrease the country's need to rely on foreign imports.

D. The agencies were formed in order to provide training to individuals so that they could become skilled laborers.

Question 7

Use the timeline and what you know about U.S. history to answer the question.

	Supreme Court Case
1954	*Brown v. Board of Education of Topeka, Kansas* rules that racial segregation in public schools is unlawful.
1962	*Bailey v. Patterson* rules that public transportation cannot enforce racial segregation and any state laws enabling this are unconstitutional.
1966	*Brown v. Louisiana* rules that protesting racial segregation in public libraries is protected under the First Amendment.
1986	*Batson v. Kentucky* rules that excluding members of the defendant's race from a jury solely based on their race denies the defendant equal protection guaranteed by the Sixth Amendment.

Which of the following **best** summarizes the primary impact of these Supreme Court case rulings on American civil rights?

A. The states combated the federal government's infringement on individuals' rights to privacy and defended their civil rights.

B. The federal government expanded the judicial system and limited the civil rights of U.S. citizens.

C. The states turned over the task of ensuring an individual's civil rights to the federal government.

D. The federal government improved and safeguarded American civil rights.

SECTION 3
MAPS, IMAGES, AND TIMELINES

Maps, Images, and Timelines Preview

Instructions

Complete the quiz. If time remains, check your answers.

Source 1

This political cartoon depicts Senator Joseph McCarthy addressing to members of HUAC with the caption "Now go get some convictions, boys." The desk between them has two piles of papers, one labeled "FAKE LETTERS and the other "DOCTORED PHOTOS"

Question 8

Based on Source 1, which statements **best** explain how the second Red Scare and McCarthyism influenced efforts to contain communism in the U.S.?

Select the **two** correct answers.

A. They contributed to a rise in protests of overseas wars.

B. They led to increased segregation in American culture.

C. They resulted in false accusations and interrogations that ruined reputations.

D. They led to the development of a more technologically advanced society.

E. They prompted fears of nuclear attack, leading some to build bomb shelters.

F. They created an investigative committee to search for communists in the country.

G. They prompted the government to increase military spending to challenge the Soviet Union.

Source 2

Immigration to the United States

Timeline of U.S. Immigration Legislation at the Turn of the 20ᵗʰ Century

1882 — The Chinese Exclusion Act is passed to block Chinese laborers from immigrating to the United States

1892 — The Geary Act extends and strengthens the Chinese Exclusion Act

1904 — The Chinese Exclusion Act is extended indefinitely

1917 — The Barred Zone Act bans immigrants from much of Asia and imposes a literacy test on other immigrants

1921 — The Emergency Quota Act restricts the annual immigration from a country to only 3% of the foreign-born population from that country in 1910

1924 — The Johnson-Reed Act completely bans immigrants from Asia and restricts the annual immigration from a country to only 2% of the current foreign-born population from that country in the United States as determined by the 1890 census

Question 9

Using Source 2, how did the passage of immigration laws between 1882 and 1924 **most likely** affect immigration patterns to the United States?

A. The average education level of incoming immigrants decreased.

B. New immigrants mainly came from countries with smaller immigrant populations in the U.S.

C. More immigrants arrived from China than from any other country.

D. Immigration from outside Europe sharply decreased.

Source 3

Political Events of the 1960s and 1970s

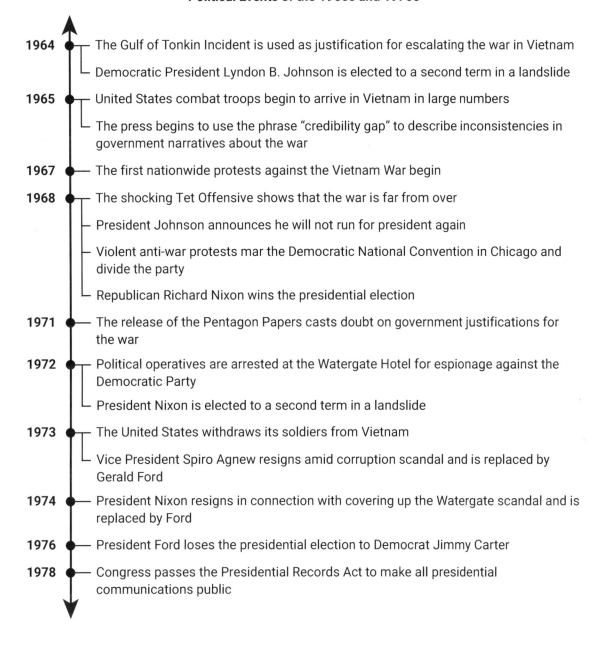

1964 — The Gulf of Tonkin Incident is used as justification for escalating the war in Vietnam

Democratic President Lyndon B. Johnson is elected to a second term in a landslide

1965 — United States combat troops begin to arrive in Vietnam in large numbers

The press begins to use the phrase "credibility gap" to describe inconsistencies in government narratives about the war

1967 — The first nationwide protests against the Vietnam War begin

1968 — The shocking Tet Offensive shows that the war is far from over

President Johnson announces he will not run for president again

Violent anti-war protests mar the Democratic National Convention in Chicago and divide the party

Republican Richard Nixon wins the presidential election

1971 — The release of the Pentagon Papers casts doubt on government justifications for the war

1972 — Political operatives are arrested at the Watergate Hotel for espionage against the Democratic Party

President Nixon is elected to a second term in a landslide

1973 — The United States withdraws its soldiers from Vietnam

Vice President Spiro Agnew resigns amid corruption scandal and is replaced by Gerald Ford

1974 — President Nixon resigns in connection with covering up the Watergate scandal and is replaced by Ford

1976 — President Ford loses the presidential election to Democrat Jimmy Carter

1978 — Congress passes the Presidential Records Act to make all presidential communications public

Source 4

Electoral Maps from 1964 and 1968

These maps show the results of two consecutive presidential elections.
Use the key to see which party each state supported in each election.

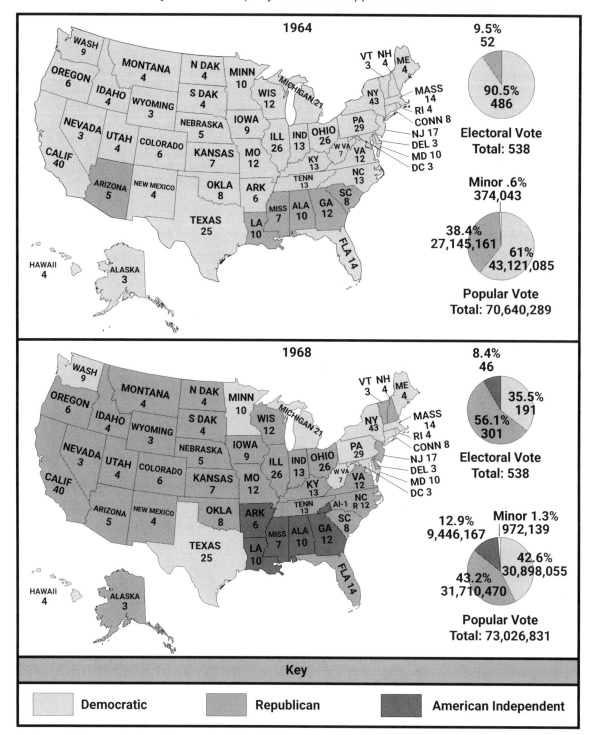

Source: Public Domain, National Atlas 2008

Question 10

Using Sources 3 and 4, which statements **best** explain why voting behavior shifted so dramatically from 1964 to 1968?

Select the **two** correct answers.

A. Congress passed the Presidential Records Act.

B. The media leaked the Pentagon Papers to the public.

C. The Johnson administration misled the public about the Vietnam War.

D. Spiro Agnew resigned from the vice presidency.

E. The Democratic Party split into quarreling factions.

F. The Gulf of Tonkin Incident was used as justification for involvement in Vietnam.

A Political Statement

Instructions

Refer to the source and question below as your instructor leads the discussion. Circle two correct answers.

Stay Inside the Lines

When you're analyzing a political cartoon, focus on what's depicted in the image. If you can't support an answer with what you see, or if you have to talk yourself through several leaps of logic to make it work, that answer is probably incorrect.

Source 1

This political cartoon depicts Senator Joseph McCarthy addressing to members of HUAC with the caption "Now go get some convictions, boys." The desk between them has two piles of papers, one labeled "FAKE LETTERS and the other "DOCTORED PHOTOS"

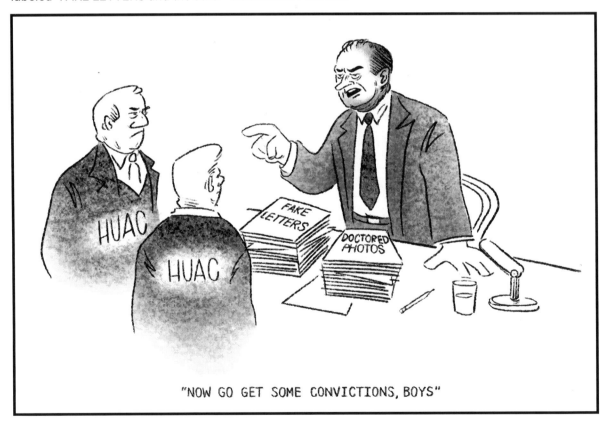

"NOW GO GET SOME CONVICTIONS, BOYS"

Question 8

Based on Source 1, which statements **best** explain how the second Red Scare and McCarthyism influenced efforts to contain communism in the U.S.?

Select the **two** correct answers.

A. They contributed to a rise in protests of overseas wars.

B. They led to increased segregation in American culture.

C. They resulted in false accusations and interrogations that ruined reputations.

D. They led to the development of a more technologically advanced society.

E. They prompted fears of nuclear attack, leading some to build bomb shelters.

F. They created an investigative committee to search for communists in the country.

G. They prompted the government to increase military spending to challenge the Soviet Union.

Timeline Gold

Instructions

Refer to the sources and question below as your instructor leads the discussion. Circle the correct answer.

Just the Highlights

The timeline is the *most* useful, straightforward source available on the LEAP U.S. History test. It gives you the most important details without much to sort through. Pick key words and dates from the question, and use them to scan the timeline for the most relevant information.

Source 2

Immigration to the United States

Timeline of U.S. Immigration Legislation at the Turn of the 20th Century

1882	The Chinese Exclusion Act is passed to block Chinese laborers from immigrating to the United States
1892	The Geary Act extends and strengthens the Chinese Exclusion Act
1904	The Chinese Exclusion Act is extended indefinitely
1917	The Barred Zone Act bans immigrants from much of Asia and imposes a literacy test on other immigrants
1921	The Emergency Quota Act restricts the annual immigration from a country to only 3% of the foreign-born population from that country in 1910
1924	The Johnson-Reed Act completely bans immigrants from Asia and restricts the annual immigration from a country to only 2% of the current foreign-born population from that country in the United States as determined by the 1890 census

Question 9

Using Source 2, how did the passage of immigration laws between 1882 and 1924 **most likely** affect immigration patterns to the United States?

A. The average education level of incoming immigrants decreased.

B. New immigrants mainly came from countries with smaller immigrant populations in the U.S.

C. More immigrants arrived from China than from any other country.

D. Immigration from outside Europe sharply decreased.

A Combination of Things

Instructions

Refer to the sources and question below as your instructor leads the discussion. Circle two correct answers.

Reference Check

When you're asked about more than one source in a single question, it means doing a little cross-referencing. The simplest of the sources (like a map or image) can clarify a key detail from a more complex source (like a passage or timeline).

To answer the question, start with the simplest source and look for where its information overlaps with other sources.

Source 3

Political Events of the 1960s and 1970s

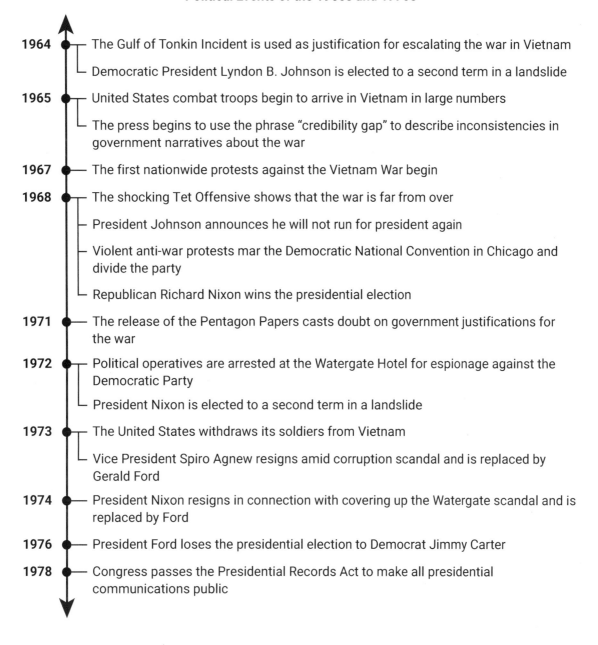

1964 — The Gulf of Tonkin Incident is used as justification for escalating the war in Vietnam

— Democratic President Lyndon B. Johnson is elected to a second term in a landslide

1965 — United States combat troops begin to arrive in Vietnam in large numbers

— The press begins to use the phrase "credibility gap" to describe inconsistencies in government narratives about the war

1967 — The first nationwide protests against the Vietnam War begin

1968 — The shocking Tet Offensive shows that the war is far from over

— President Johnson announces he will not run for president again

— Violent anti-war protests mar the Democratic National Convention in Chicago and divide the party

— Republican Richard Nixon wins the presidential election

1971 — The release of the Pentagon Papers casts doubt on government justifications for the war

1972 — Political operatives are arrested at the Watergate Hotel for espionage against the Democratic Party

— President Nixon is elected to a second term in a landslide

1973 — The United States withdraws its soldiers from Vietnam

— Vice President Spiro Agnew resigns amid corruption scandal and is replaced by Gerald Ford

1974 — President Nixon resigns in connection with covering up the Watergate scandal and is replaced by Ford

1976 — President Ford loses the presidential election to Democrat Jimmy Carter

1978 — Congress passes the Presidential Records Act to make all presidential communications public

Source 4

Electoral Maps from 1964 and 1968

These maps show the results of two consecutive presidential elections.
Use the key to see which party each state supported in each election.

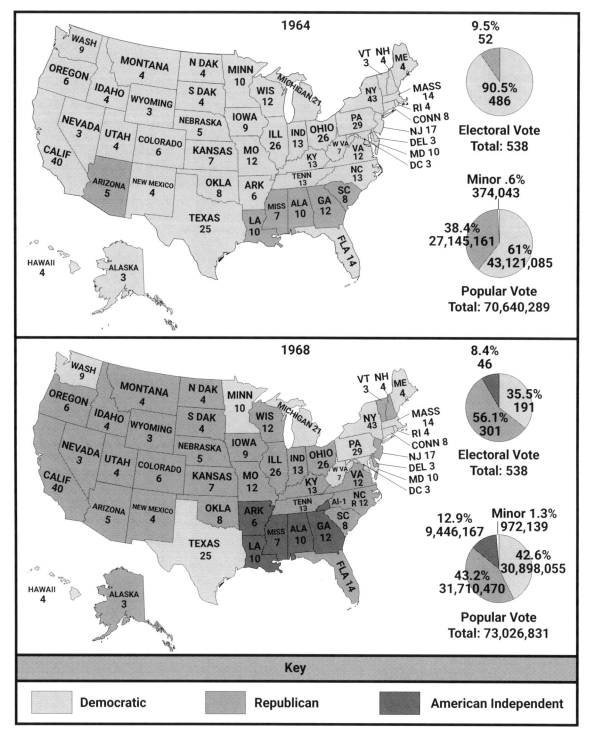

Source: Public Domain, National Atlas 2008

Question 10

Using Sources 3 and 4, which statements **best** explain why voting behavior shifted so dramatically from 1964 to 1968?

Select the **two** correct answers.

A. Congress passed the Presidential Records Act.

B. The media leaked the Pentagon Papers to the public.

C. The Johnson administration misled the public about the Vietnam War.

D. Spiro Agnew resigned from the vice presidency.

E. The Democratic Party split into quarreling factions.

F. The Gulf of Tonkin Incident was used as justification for involvement in Vietnam.

Test Run

Instructions

Complete the quiz. If time remains, check your answers.

Source 1

This political cartoon shows President Richard Nixon, depicted as a police officer, arresting a figure labeled "Freedom of the Press" as part of the "Pentagon Papers Investigation."

"I found the culprit!"

Question 11

Based on Source 1, which statement **best** explains how the Pentagon Papers scandal affected the federal government?

A. The leaking of secret government documents reduced partisanship in the government.

B. The controversy surrounding the Pentagon Papers strengthened the government's commitment to transparency.

C. The leaking of secret government documents increased the government's protection of whistleblowers.

D. The controversy surrounding the Pentagon Papers motivated the government to attempt to censor the media.

Source 2

Events Related to Terrorism and the War on Terror

1988 — Osama bin Laden and others found Al-Qaeda in Pakistan

1989 — The Soviet Union ends its occupation of Afghanistan after facing stiff resistance from U.S.-backed rebels, leaving a power vacuum

1990 — Iraq, under Saddam Hussein, invades the neighboring country of Kuwait

1991 — A coalition led by the United States defends Kuwait and defeats Iraq during the Persian Gulf War

1993 — Terrorists bomb the World Trade Center in New York City

1994 — The Taliban begin their rise to power during the Afghan Civil War

1996 — The Taliban take control of the Afghan capital and establish the Islamic Emirate of Afghanistan

— Osama bin Laden and other Al-Qaeda leaders relocate from Sudan to Afghanistan

2000 — Al-Qaeda terrorists bomb the *USS Cole* in Yemen

2001 — On September 11, Al-Qaeda terrorists destroy the World Trade Center and damage the Pentagon in Washington, D.C., in a series of coordinated attacks using hijacked aircraft

— Congress passes the Patriot Act

— The United States government expands the scope of phone-tapping laws to thwart terrorism

— The United States sends forces to Afghanistan to topple the Taliban and expel Al-Qaeda leaders, including Osama bin Laden

— The Transportation Security Administration (TSA) is created to monitor travel

2002 — President George W. Bush creates the Department of Homeland Security

2003 — The United States sends forces to Iraq, which it accuses of sponsoring terrorism and having weapons of mass destruction, and ends the Hussein regime

2011 — Osama bin Laden is killed in a U.S. military raid in Pakistan

— The Iraq War comes to an end as the United States completes the withdrawal of its forces

2013 — The terrorist group known as the Islamic State of Iraq and Syria (ISIS) begins a campaign to retake Iraq

2014 — United States military forces return to Iraq to fight against ISIS

2015 — Congress passes the USA FREEDOM Act to renew the Patriot Act while also limiting the surveillance of American citizens

Question 12

Based on Source 2, which statement **best** explains how the September 11, 2001, terrorist attacks affected U.S. relations in the Middle East?

A. Iraq provided military assistance to the United States against terrorist groups.

B. The United States deployed its military to Afghanistan to eliminate terrorist groups.

C. The United States supported a revolution in Iraq to overthrow the government.

D. The United States supplied arms and resources to military groups in Afghanistan.

SECTION 4
THE PASSAGES

The Passages Preview

Instructions

Complete the quiz. If time remains, check your answers.

Source 1

Excerpt from "The Biography of a Chinaman" (1903)

by Lee Chew

This excerpt is from a magazine article about the life of a Chinese immigrant in the United States.

I worked on my father's farm till I was about sixteen years of age, when a man of our tribe came back from America and took ground as large as four city blocks and made a paradise of it . . .

The man had gone away from our village a poor boy. Now he returned with unlimited wealth, which he had obtained in the country of the American wizards . . .

The wealth of this man filled my mind with the idea that I, too, would like to go to the country of the wizards and gain some of their wealth, and after a long time my father consented, and gave me his blessing . . .

When I got to San Francisco, which was before the Exclusion Act . . . A man got me work as a house servant in an American family, and my start was the same as that of almost all the Chinese in this country . . .

When I first opened a laundry it was in company with a partner, who had been in the business for some years. We went to a town about 500 miles inland, where a railroad was building. We got a board shanty[1] and worked for the men employed by the railroads . . . We had to put up with many insults and some frauds, as men would come in and claim parcels that did not belong to them, saying they had lost their tickets, and would fight if they did not get what they asked for. Sometimes we were taken before Magistrates[2] and fined for losing shirts that we had never seen . . .

The reason why so many Chinese go into the laundry business in this country is because it requires little capital[3] and is one of the few opportunities that are open. Men of other nationalities who are jealous of the Chinese, because he is a more faithful worker than one of their people, have raised such a great outcry about Chinese cheap labor that they have shut him out of working on farms or in factories or building railroads or making streets or digging sewers. He cannot practice any trade, and his opportunities to do business are limited to his own countrymen. So he opens a laundry when he quits domestic service . . .

More than half the Chinese in this country would become citizens if allowed to do so, and would be patriotic Americans. But how can they make this country their home as matters now are! They are not allowed to bring wives here from China, and if they marry American women there is a great outcry . . .

Under the circumstances, how can I call this my home, and how can any one blame me if I take my money and go back to my village in China?

¹**shanty:** small shack

²**Magistrates:** judges

³**capital:** starting money

Question 13

Which statement **best** explains how the reception of Chinese immigrants to the United States of America was reflected in legislation shown in Source 1?

A. American citizens encouraged lawmakers to create incentives for immigrants to come to the United States.

B. American citizens promoted legislation that allowed immigrants to start their own businesses.

C. American citizens supported laws designed to prevent immigrants from competing for their jobs.

D. American citizens wanted the government to decrease restrictions on immigration.

Question 14

Based on Source 1, which statement **best** reflects the experience of Chinese immigrants who arrived in the United States in the 1800s?

A. Chinese immigrants mainly found employment in the skilled trades.

B. Chinese immigrants relied on one another for economic opportunities.

C. Chinese immigrants severed all connections with their native culture.

D. Chinese immigrants moved inland to purchase land for agricultural purposes.

Source 1

Excerpt from "The Biography of a Chinaman" (1903)

by Lee Chew

This excerpt is from a magazine article about the life of a Chinese immigrant in the United States.

I worked on my father's farm till I was about sixteen years of age, when a man of our tribe came back from America and took ground as large as four city blocks and made a paradise of it . . .

The man had gone away from our village a poor boy. Now he returned with unlimited wealth, which he had obtained in the country of the American wizards . . .

The wealth of this man filled my mind with the idea that I, too, would like to go to the country of the wizards and gain some of their wealth, and after a long time my father consented, and gave me his blessing . . .

When I got to San Francisco, which was before the Exclusion Act . . . A man got me work as a house servant in an American family, and my start was the same as that of almost all the Chinese in this country . . .

When I first opened a laundry it was in company with a partner, who had been in the business for some years. We went to a town about 500 miles inland, where a railroad was building. We got a board shanty[1] and worked for the men employed by the railroads . . . We had to put up with many insults and some frauds, as men would come in and claim parcels that did not belong to them, saying they had lost their tickets, and would fight if they did not get what they asked for. Sometimes we were taken before Magistrates[2] and fined for losing shirts that we had never seen . . .

The reason why so many Chinese go into the laundry business in this country is because it requires little capital[3] and is one of the few opportunities that are open. Men of other nationalities who are jealous of the Chinese, because he is a more faithful worker than one of their people, have raised such a great outcry about Chinese cheap labor that they have shut him out of working on farms or in factories or building railroads or making streets or digging sewers. He cannot practice any trade, and his opportunities to do business are limited to his own countrymen. So he opens a laundry when he quits domestic service . . .

More than half the Chinese in this country would become citizens if allowed to do so, and would be patriotic Americans. But how can they make this country their home as matters now are! They are not allowed to bring wives here from China, and if they marry American women there is a great outcry . . .

Under the circumstances, how can I call this my home, and how can any one blame me if I take my money and go back to my village in China?

---

[1]**shanty:** small shack

[2]**Magistrates:** judges

[3]**capital:** starting money

Source 2

Welcome to All! (1880)

This political cartoon shows immigrants fleeing a cloud labeled "war" and boarding the "U.S. Ark of Refuge," which features signs saying "free education," "free land," "free speech," "free ballot," "free lunch," "no oppressive taxes," "no expensive kings," "no compulsory military service," and "no knouts[1] or dungeons." The caption reads "WELCOME TO ALL!"

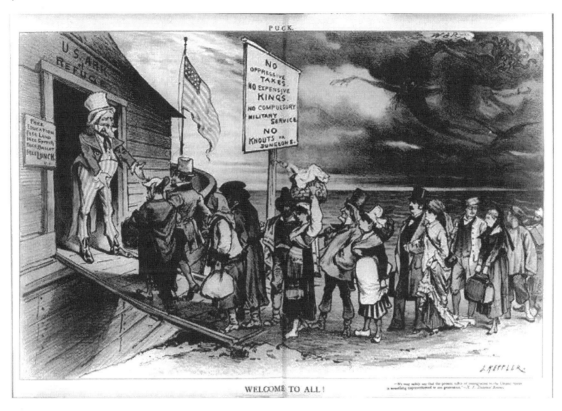

Source: J. Keppler, 1880. Library of Congress Collection.

[1] **knouts:** whips used for punishment

Question 15

Based on Sources 1 and 2, which statement **best** explains how popular portrayals of immigration to the United States differed from the actual experience of immigrants in the late nineteenth century?

A. The United States was supposed to be a land of peace, but immigrants were forced to fight in foreign wars.

B. The United States was supposed to be a land of opportunity, but immigrants had limited employment prospects.

C. The United States was supposed to allow free expression, but immigrants were not allowed to talk about their problems.

D. The United States economy was supposed to be open, but immigrants were barred from starting their own businesses.

What's the Big Idea?

Instructions

Refer to the source and question below as your instructor leads the discussion. Circle the correct answer.

Main Idea

Questions about passages are more about reading than memorizing historical facts. Start with the main idea of the passage. Eliminate answers that don't match what the author says.

Source 1

Excerpt from "The Biography of a Chinaman" (1903)

by Lee Chew

This excerpt is from a magazine article about the life of a Chinese immigrant in the United States.

I worked on my father's farm till I was about sixteen years of age, when a man of our tribe came back from America and took ground as large as four city blocks and made a paradise of it . . .

The man had gone away from our village a poor boy. Now he returned with unlimited wealth, which he had obtained in the country of the American wizards . . .

The wealth of this man filled my mind with the idea that I, too, would like to go to the country of the wizards and gain some of their wealth, and after a long time my father consented, and gave me his blessing . . .

When I got to San Francisco, which was before the Exclusion Act . . . A man got me work as a house servant in an American family, and my start was the same as that of almost all the Chinese in this country . . .

When I first opened a laundry it was in company with a partner, who had been in the business for some years. We went to a town about 500 miles inland, where a railroad was building. We got a board shanty[1] and worked for the men employed by the railroads . . . We had to put up with many insults and some frauds, as men would come in and claim parcels that did not belong to them, saying they had lost their tickets, and would fight if they did not get what they asked for. Sometimes we were taken before Magistrates[2] and fined for losing shirts that we had never seen . . .

The reason why so many Chinese go into the laundry business in this country is because it requires little capital[3] and is one of the few opportunities that are open. Men of other nationalities who are jealous of the Chinese, because he is a more faithful worker than one of their people, have raised such a great outcry about Chinese cheap labor that they have shut him out of working on farms or in factories or building railroads or making streets or digging sewers. He cannot practice any trade, and his opportunities to do business are limited to his own countrymen. So he opens a laundry when he quits domestic service . . .

More than half the Chinese in this country would become citizens if allowed to do so, and would be patriotic Americans. But how can they make this country their home as matters now are! They are not allowed to bring wives here from China, and if they marry American women there is a great outcry . . .

Under the circumstances, how can I call this my home, and how can any one blame me if I take my money and go back to my village in China?

[1] **shanty:** small shack

[2] **Magistrates:** judges

[3] **capital:** starting money

Question 13

Which statement **best** explains how the reception of Chinese immigrants to the United States of America was reflected in legislation shown in Source 1?

A. American citizens encouraged lawmakers to create incentives for immigrants to come to the United States.

B. American citizens promoted legislation that allowed immigrants to start their own businesses.

C. American citizens supported laws designed to prevent immigrants from competing for their jobs.

D. American citizens wanted the government to decrease restrictions on immigration.

Detail-Oriented

Instructions

Refer to the source and question below as your instructor leads the discussion. Circle the correct answer.

Trap Answers

Some passage questions focus more on the details than on the main idea of the passage. When you run into a question like that, expect to see some typical trap answers:

- **Recycled Words,** which repeat words or phrases from the passage in an inaccurate way.

- **Outliers,** which bring up a new topic not mentioned in the passage.

- **Opposites,** which say the exact opposite of what's said in the passage.

Source 1

Excerpt from "The Biography of a Chinaman" (1903)

by Lee Chew

This excerpt is from a magazine article about the life of a Chinese immigrant in the United States.

I worked on my father's farm till I was about sixteen years of age, when a man of our tribe came back from America and took ground as large as four city blocks and made a paradise of it . . .

The man had gone away from our village a poor boy. Now he returned with unlimited wealth, which he had obtained in the country of the American wizards . . .

The wealth of this man filled my mind with the idea that I, too, would like to go to the country of the wizards and gain some of their wealth, and after a long time my father consented, and gave me his blessing . . .

When I got to San Francisco, which was before the Exclusion Act . . . A man got me work as a house servant in an American family, and my start was the same as that of almost all the Chinese in this country . . .

When I first opened a laundry it was in company with a partner, who had been in the business for some years. We went to a town about 500 miles inland, where a railroad was building. We got a board shanty[1] and worked for the men employed by the railroads . . . We had to put up with many insults and some frauds, as men would come in and claim parcels that did not belong to them, saying they had lost their tickets, and would fight if they did not get what they asked for. Sometimes we were taken before Magistrates[2] and fined for losing shirts that we had never seen . . .

The reason why so many Chinese go into the laundry business in this country is because it requires little capital[3] and is one of the few opportunities that are open. Men of other nationalities who are jealous of the Chinese, because he is a more faithful worker than one of their people, have raised such a great outcry about Chinese cheap labor that they have shut him out of working on farms or in factories or building railroads or making streets or digging sewers. He cannot practice any trade, and his opportunities to do business are limited to his own countrymen. So he opens a laundry when he quits domestic service . . .

More than half the Chinese in this country would become citizens if allowed to do so, and would be patriotic Americans. But how can they make this country their home as matters now are! They are not allowed to bring wives here from China, and if they marry American women there is a great outcry . . .

Under the circumstances, how can I call this my home, and how can any one blame me if I take my money and go back to my village in China?

[1] **shanty:** small shack

[2] **Magistrates:** judges

[3] **capital:** starting money

Question 14

Based on Source 1, which statement **best** reflects the experience of Chinese immigrants who arrived in the United States in the 1800s?

A. Chinese immigrants mainly found employment in the skilled trades.

B. Chinese immigrants relied on one another for economic opportunities.

C. Chinese immigrants severed all connections with their native culture.

D. Chinese immigrants moved inland to purchase land for agricultural purposes.

This page intentionally left blank. Content resumes on the next page.

Maps, Images, and Timelines Reboot

Instructions

Use what you know about timelines to answer the question below.

Source 3

Events Related to Terrorism and the War on Terror

1988 — Osama bin Laden and others found Al-Qaeda in Pakistan

1989 — The Soviet Union ends its occupation of Afghanistan after facing stiff resistance from U.S.-backed rebels, leaving a power vacuum

1990 — Iraq, under Saddam Hussein, invades the neighboring country of Kuwait

1991 — A coalition led by the United States defends Kuwait and defeats Iraq during the Persian Gulf War

1993 — Terrorists bomb the World Trade Center in New York City

1994 — The Taliban begin their rise to power during the Afghan Civil War

1996 — The Taliban take control of the Afghan capital and establish the Islamic Emirate of Afghanistan

— Osama bin Laden and other Al-Qaeda leaders relocate from Sudan to Afghanistan

2000 — Al-Qaeda terrorists bomb the *USS Cole* in Yemen

2001 — On September 11, Al-Qaeda terrorists destroy the World Trade Center and damage the Pentagon in Washington, D.C., in a series of coordinated attacks using hijacked aircraft

— Congress passes the Patriot Act

— The United States government expands the scope of phone-tapping laws to thwart terrorism

— The United States sends forces to Afghanistan to topple the Taliban and expel Al-Qaeda leaders, including Osama bin Laden

— The Transportation Security Administration (TSA) is created to monitor travel

2002 — President George W. Bush creates the Department of Homeland Security

2003 — The United States sends forces to Iraq, which it accuses of sponsoring terrorism and having weapons of mass destruction, and ends the Hussein regime

2011 — Osama bin Laden is killed in a U.S. military raid in Pakistan

— The Iraq War comes to an end as the United States completes the withdrawal of its forces

2013 — The terrorist group known as the Islamic State of Iraq and Syria (ISIS) begins a campaign to retake Iraq

2014 — United States military forces return to Iraq to fight against ISIS

2015 — Congress passes the USA FREEDOM Act to renew the Patriot Act while also limiting the surveillance of American citizens

Using Source 3, which statement explains how the Patriot Act **most likely** affected the role of the federal government?

A. The federal government increased its surveillance activities at home and abroad.

B. The federal government expanded its participation in military actions abroad.

C. The federal government ended its cooperation with foreign intelligence services.

D. The federal government delegated more power to local governments.

Combining Your Resources

Instructions

Refer to the sources and question below as your instructor leads the discussion. Circle the correct answer.

Basics First

When you're asked about multiple resources, start with the more basic of the two to see if you can eliminate any answers. Then tackle the more complex source to help you decide between your remaining options.

Source 1

Excerpt from "The Biography of a Chinaman" (1903)

by Lee Chew

This excerpt is from a magazine article about the life of a Chinese immigrant in the United States.

I worked on my father's farm till I was about sixteen years of age, when a man of our tribe came back from America and took ground as large as four city blocks and made a paradise of it . . .

The man had gone away from our village a poor boy. Now he returned with unlimited wealth, which he had obtained in the country of the American wizards . . .

The wealth of this man filled my mind with the idea that I, too, would like to go to the country of the wizards and gain some of their wealth, and after a long time my father consented, and gave me his blessing . . .

When I got to San Francisco, which was before the Exclusion Act . . . A man got me work as a house servant in an American family, and my start was the same as that of almost all the Chinese in this country . . .

When I first opened a laundry it was in company with a partner, who had been in the business for some years. We went to a town about 500 miles inland, where a railroad was building. We got a board shanty[1] and worked for the men employed by the railroads . . . We had to put up with many insults and some frauds, as men would come in and claim parcels that did not belong to them, saying they had lost their tickets, and would fight if they did not get what they asked for. Sometimes we were taken before Magistrates[2] and fined for losing shirts that we had never seen . . .

The reason why so many Chinese go into the laundry business in this country is because it requires little capital[3] and is one of the few opportunities that are open. Men of other nationalities who are jealous of the Chinese, because he is a more faithful worker than one of their people, have raised such a great outcry about Chinese cheap labor that they have shut him out of working on farms or in factories or building railroads or making streets or digging sewers. He cannot practice any trade, and his opportunities to do business are limited to his own countrymen. So he opens a laundry when he quits domestic service . . .

More than half the Chinese in this country would become citizens if allowed to do so, and would be patriotic Americans. But how can they make this country their home as matters now are! They are not allowed to bring wives here from China, and if they marry American women there is a great outcry . . .

Under the circumstances, how can I call this my home, and how can any one blame me if I take my money and go back to my village in China?

[1]**shanty:** small shack

[2]**Magistrates:** judges

[3]**capital:** starting money

Source 2

Welcome to All! (1880)

This political cartoon shows immigrants fleeing a cloud labeled "war" and boarding the "U.S. Ark of Refuge," which features signs saying "free education," "free land," "free speech," "free ballot," "free lunch," "no oppressive taxes," "no expensive kings," "no compulsory military service," and "no knouts[1] or dungeons." The caption reads "WELCOME TO ALL!"

Source: J. Keppler, 1880. Library of Congress Collection.

[1]**knouts:** whips used for punishment

Question 15

Based on Sources 1 and 2, which statement **best** explains how popular portrayals of immigration to the United States differed from the actual experience of immigrants in the late nineteenth century?

A. The United States was supposed to be a land of peace, but immigrants were forced to fight in foreign wars.

B. The United States was supposed to be a land of opportunity, but immigrants had limited employment prospects.

C. The United States was supposed to allow free expression, but immigrants were not allowed to talk about their problems.

D. The United States economy was supposed to be open, but immigrants were barred from starting their own businesses.

Test Run

Instructions

Complete the quiz. If time remains, check your answers.

Source 1

Excerpt from the European Recovery Act/Marshall Plan

This excerpt is from section 102 of the European Recovery Act from the second session of Congress, January 6, 1948.

(a) Recognizing the intimate economic and other relationships between the United States and the nations of Europe endangers the establishment of a lasting peace, the general welfare and national interest of the United States, and the attainment of the objectives of the United Nations.

The restoration or maintenance in European countries of principles of individual liberty, free institutions, and genuine independence rests largely upon the establishment of sound economic conditions, stable international economic relationships, and the achievement by the countries of Europe of a healthy economy independent of extraordinary outside assistance.

The accomplishment of these objectives calls for a plan of European recovery, open to all such nations which cooperate in such plan, based upon a strong production effort, the expansion of foreign trade, the creation and maintenance of internal financial stability, and the development of economic cooperation, including all possible steps to establish and maintain equitable rates of exchange and to bring about the progressive elimination of trade barriers.

Map of Cold War–era Europe showing countries that received Marshall Plan aid. The columns show the relative amount of total aid per nation.

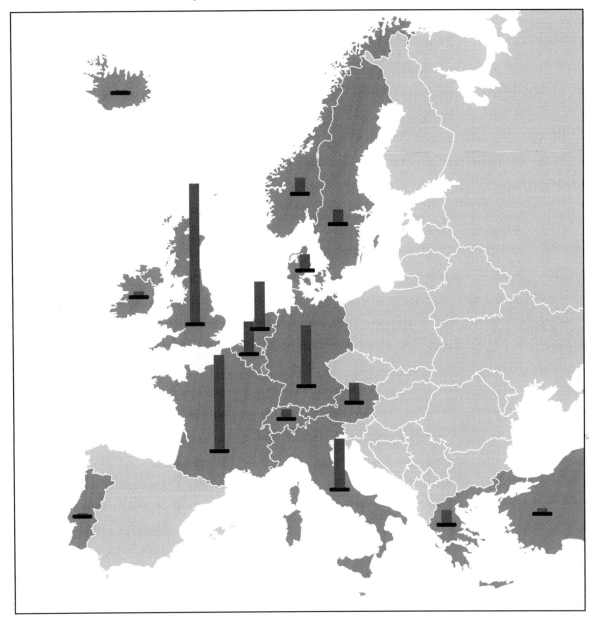

Question 16

Based on Source 1, which statement **best** explains how the Marshall Plan reflected the policy of containment in the post–World War II world?

A. The Marshall Plan provided military support to European nations to prevent the spread of communism.

B. The Marshall Plan provided monetary support to European nations to rebuild and to stop communism from spreading.

C. The Marshall Plan formed an organization of alliances between countries to help each other in case of an attack by the Soviet Union.

D. The Marshall Plan allowed democratic nations to provide supplies to their citizens blockaded by the Soviet Union.

Source 2

Excerpt from "Address to the Nation on the War in Vietnam" (1969)

by President Richard Nixon

This excerpt is from a 1969 speech given by President Richard Nixon on the status of the Vietnam War.

Tonight I want to talk to you on a subject of deep concern to all Americans and to many people in all parts of the world—the war in Vietnam.

I believe that one of the reasons for the deep division about Vietnam is that many Americans have lost confidence in what their Government has told them about our policy. The American people cannot and should not be asked to support a policy which involves the overriding issues of war and peace unless they know the truth about that policy.

Tonight, therefore, I would like to answer some of the questions that I know are on the minds of many of you listening to me.

. . . We have adopted a plan which we have worked out in cooperation with the South Vietnamese for the complete withdrawal of all U.S. combat ground forces, and their replacement by South Vietnamese forces on an orderly scheduled timetable.

This withdrawal will be made from strength and not from weakness. As South Vietnamese forces become stronger, the rate of American withdrawal can become greater.

Question 17

Using Source 2, which statement **best** describes the social causes of Nixon's plan of withdrawal from Vietnam in the 1970s?

A. The Moral Majority became more active in American politics.

B. The South Vietnamese forces advocated for a surrender to North Vietnam.

C. Congress approved the U.S. to take all necessary measures to repel communism in Vietnam.

D. There were widespread public protests against U.S. involvement in Vietnam.

Question 18

Seven phrases are highlighted in the excerpt from "The Biography of a Chinaman." From these phrases, select the **four** correct phrases that **best** reflect reasons why the author, Lee Chew, wanted to "take my money and go back to my village in China." Underline your answers.

I worked on my father's farm till I was about sixteen years of age, when a man of our tribe came back from America and took ground as large as four city blocks and made a paradise of it . . .

The man had gone away from our village a poor boy. Now he returned with unlimited wealth, which he had obtained in the country of the American wizards . . .

The wealth of this man filled my mind with the idea that I, too, would like to go to the country of the wizards and gain some of their wealth, and after a long time my father consented, and gave me his blessing . . .

When I got to San Francisco, which was before the Exclusion Act . . . A man got me work as a house servant in an American family, and my start was the same as that of almost all the Chinese in this country . . .

When I first opened a laundry it was in company with a partner, who had been in the business for some years. We went to a town about 500 miles inland, where a railroad was building. We got a board shanty[1] and worked for the men employed by the railroads . . . We had to put up with many insults and some frauds, as men would come in and claim parcels that did not belong to them, saying they had lost their tickets, and would fight if they did not get what they asked for. Sometimes we were taken before Magistrates[2] and fined for losing shirts that we had never seen . . .

The reason why so many Chinese go into the laundry business in this country is because it requires little capital[3] and is one of the few opportunities that are open. Men of other nationalities who are jealous of the Chinese, because he is a more faithful worker than one of their people, have raised such a great outcry about Chinese cheap labor that they have shut him out of working on farms or in factories or building railroads or making streets or digging sewers. He cannot practice any trade, and his opportunities to do business are limited to his own countrymen. So he opens a laundry when he quits domestic service . . .

More than half the Chinese in this country would become citizens if allowed to do so, and would be patriotic Americans. But how can they make this country their home as matters now are! They are not allowed to bring wives here from China, and if they marry American women there is a great outcry . . .

Under the circumstances, how can I call this my home, and how can any one blame me if I take my money and go back to my village in China?

[1]**shanty:** small shack

[2]**Magistrates:** judges

[3]**capital:** starting money

TECH-ENHANCED QUESTIONS

Tech-Enhanced Questions Preview

Instructions

Complete the quiz. If time remains, check your answers.

Source 1

Events Related to Terrorism and the War on Terror

1988 — Osama bin Laden and others found Al-Qaeda in Pakistan

1989 — The Soviet Union ends its occupation of Afghanistan after facing stiff resistance from U.S.-backed rebels, leaving a power vacuum

1990 — Iraq, under Saddam Hussein, invades the neighboring country of Kuwait

1991 — A coalition led by the United States defends Kuwait and defeats Iraq during the Persian Gulf War

1993 — Terrorists bomb the World Trade Center in New York City

1994 — The Taliban begin their rise to power during the Afghan Civil War

1996 — The Taliban take control of the Afghan capital and establish the Islamic Emirate of Afghanistan

— Osama bin Laden and other Al-Qaeda leaders relocate from Sudan to Afghanistan

2000 — Al-Qaeda terrorists bomb the *USS Cole* in Yemen

2001 — On September 11, Al-Qaeda terrorists destroy the World Trade Center and damage the Pentagon in Washington, D.C., in a series of coordinated attacks using hijacked aircraft

— Congress passes the Patriot Act

— The United States government expands the scope of phone-tapping laws to thwart terrorism

— The United States sends forces to Afghanistan to topple the Taliban and expel Al-Qaeda leaders, including Osama bin Laden

— The Transportation Security Administration (TSA) is created to monitor travel

2002 — President George W. Bush creates the Department of Homeland Security

2003 — The United States sends forces to Iraq, which it accuses of sponsoring terrorism and having weapons of mass destruction, and ends the Hussein regime

2011 — Osama bin Laden is killed in a U.S. military raid in Pakistan

— The Iraq War comes to an end as the United States completes the withdrawal of its forces

2013 — The terrorist group known as the Islamic State of Iraq and Syria (ISIS) begins a campaign to retake Iraq

2014 — United States military forces return to Iraq to fight against ISIS

2015 — Congress passes the USA FREEDOM Act to renew the Patriot Act while also limiting the surveillance of American citizens

The War on Terror

This map shows countries in which the United States has conducted major operations related to the War on Terror since 2001, including the year of the beginning of each operation.

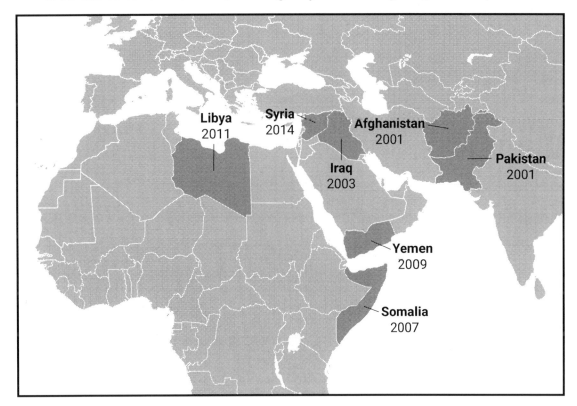

Question 19

Terrorist attacks against the United States had significant effects on U.S. foreign policy. Use the numbers in the flowchart to label the **four** relevant events below that show the effects of these attacks on U.S. foreign policy. Pay attention to chronological order.

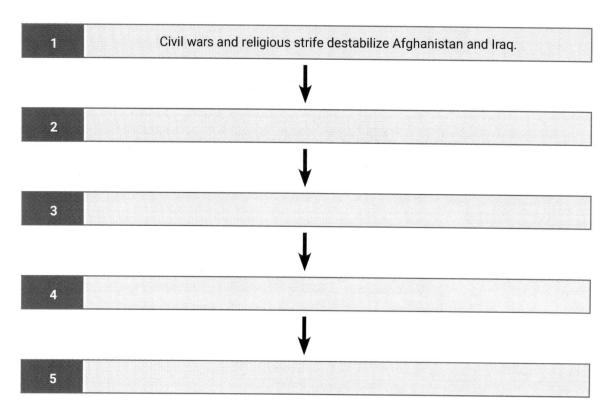

| 1 | Civil wars and religious strife destabilize Afghanistan and Iraq. |

| 2 | |

| 3 | |

| 4 | |

| 5 | |

_____ The United States military enacts a policy of non-involvement in the Middle East.

_____ Seeking to reduce instability in Iraq, the United States commits additional troops to its occupation of the region.

_____ The Taliban are deposed as leaders of Afghanistan by the United States and replaced with a new government.

_____ The United States invades Iraq, claiming its government possesses WMDs and are tied to Al-Qaeda.

_____ Taliban-linked terrorist group Al-Qaeda organizes a coordinated attack against the United States on September 11, 2001.

_____ Afghanistan and Iraq appeal to the United States for help.

Source 2

Excerpt from "Address to the Nation About the Watergate Investigations" (1973)

by President Richard Nixon

This excerpt is from a speech given by President Richard Nixon to address the Watergate scandal.

In recent months, members of my Administration and officials of the Committee for the Re-Election of the President—including some of my closest friends and most trusted aides—have been charged with involvement in what has come to be known as the Watergate affair. These include charges of illegal activity during and preceding the 1972 Presidential election and charges that responsible officials participated in efforts to cover up that illegal activity . . .

Today, in one of the most difficult decisions of my Presidency, I accepted the resignations of two of my closest associates in the White House—Bob Haldeman, John Ehrlichman—two of the finest public servants it has been my privilege to know . . .

Whatever may appear to have been the case before, whatever improper activities may yet be discovered in connection with this whole sordid[1] affair, I want the American people, I want you to know beyond the shadow of a doubt that during my term as President, justice will be pursued fairly, fully, and impartially, no matter who is involved. This office is a sacred trust, and I am determined to be worthy of that trust.

Looking back at the history of this case, two questions arise:

How could it have happened?

Who is to blame? . . .

I will not place the blame on subordinates—on people whose zeal exceeded their judgment and who may have done wrong in a cause they deeply believed to be right.

In any organization, the man at the top must bear the responsibility. That responsibility, therefore, belongs here, in this office. I accept it. And I pledge to you tonight, from this office, that I will do everything in my power to ensure that the guilty are brought to justice and that such abuses are purged from our political processes in the years to come, long after I have left this office.

Some people, quite properly appalled at the abuses that occurred, will say that Watergate demonstrates the bankruptcy of the American political system. I believe precisely the opposite is true.

[1] **sordid:** scandalous

Source 3

Political Events of the 1960s and 1970s

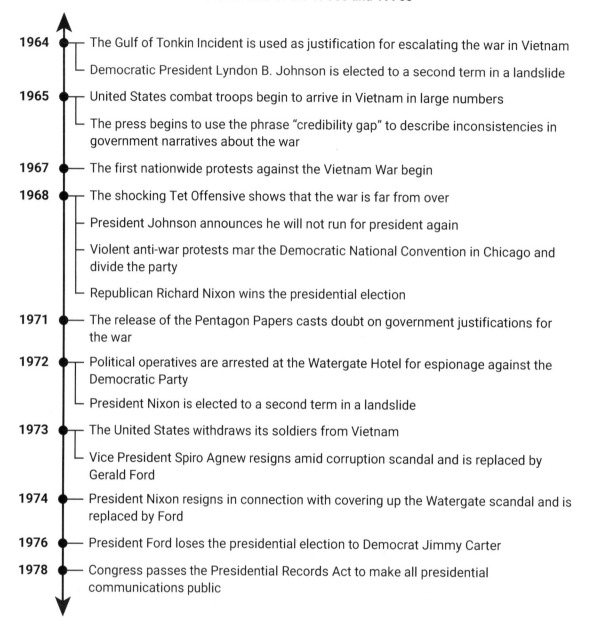

1964 — The Gulf of Tonkin Incident is used as justification for escalating the war in Vietnam

Democratic President Lyndon B. Johnson is elected to a second term in a landslide

1965 — United States combat troops begin to arrive in Vietnam in large numbers

The press begins to use the phrase "credibility gap" to describe inconsistencies in government narratives about the war

1967 — The first nationwide protests against the Vietnam War begin

1968 — The shocking Tet Offensive shows that the war is far from over

President Johnson announces he will not run for president again

Violent anti-war protests mar the Democratic National Convention in Chicago and divide the party

Republican Richard Nixon wins the presidential election

1971 — The release of the Pentagon Papers casts doubt on government justifications for the war

1972 — Political operatives are arrested at the Watergate Hotel for espionage against the Democratic Party

President Nixon is elected to a second term in a landslide

1973 — The United States withdraws its soldiers from Vietnam

Vice President Spiro Agnew resigns amid corruption scandal and is replaced by Gerald Ford

1974 — President Nixon resigns in connection with covering up the Watergate scandal and is replaced by Ford

1976 — President Ford loses the presidential election to Democrat Jimmy Carter

1978 — Congress passes the Presidential Records Act to make all presidential communications public

Question 20

The Watergate scandal had many causes and was responsible for several effects on American society. Write C for Cause or E for Effect in front of the corresponding answer choices. Choose **two** causes and **two** effects of the Watergate scandal.

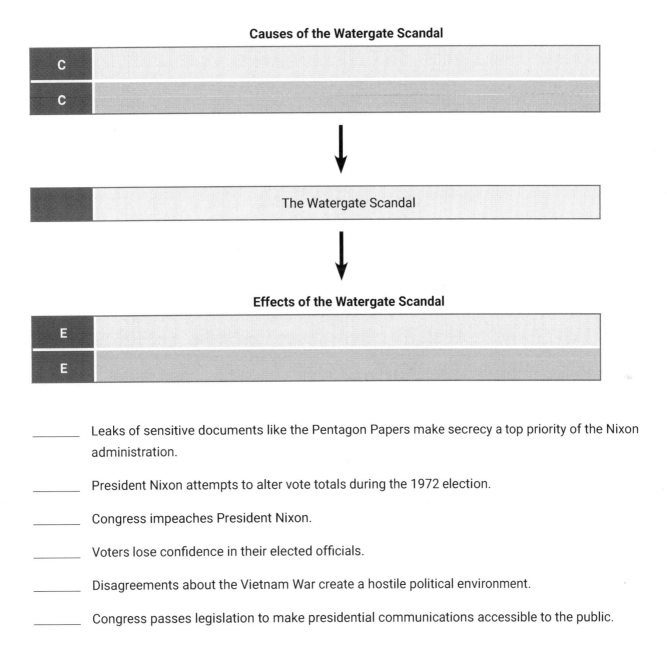

Causes of the Watergate Scandal

C	
C	

↓

The Watergate Scandal

↓

Effects of the Watergate Scandal

E	
E	

_____ Leaks of sensitive documents like the Pentagon Papers make secrecy a top priority of the Nixon administration.

_____ President Nixon attempts to alter vote totals during the 1972 election.

_____ Congress impeaches President Nixon.

_____ Voters lose confidence in their elected officials.

_____ Disagreements about the Vietnam War create a hostile political environment.

_____ Congress passes legislation to make presidential communications accessible to the public.

The Timeline Is King

Instructions

Refer to the source and question below as your instructor leads the discussion. Label your answers based on where they should be placed in the sequence.

Picking the Right Resource

Tech-enhanced questions are either the last or second-to-last question of an item set, and they *never* tell you which resource to use. If a timeline is available, use that first every time. Most often, you can answer the entire question using just the timeline.

Source 1

Events Related to Terrorism and the War on Terror

1988 — Osama bin Laden and others found Al-Qaeda in Pakistan

1989 — The Soviet Union ends its occupation of Afghanistan after facing stiff resistance from U.S.-backed rebels, leaving a power vacuum

1990 — Iraq, under Saddam Hussein, invades the neighboring country of Kuwait

1991 — A coalition led by the United States defends Kuwait and defeats Iraq during the Persian Gulf War

1993 — Terrorists bomb the World Trade Center in New York City

1994 — The Taliban begin their rise to power during the Afghan Civil War

1996 — The Taliban take control of the Afghan capital and establish the Islamic Emirate of Afghanistan

— Osama bin Laden and other Al-Qaeda leaders relocate from Sudan to Afghanistan

2000 — Al-Qaeda terrorists bomb the *USS Cole* in Yemen

2001 — On September 11, Al-Qaeda terrorists destroy the World Trade Center and damage the Pentagon in Washington, D.C., in a series of coordinated attacks using hijacked aircraft

— Congress passes the Patriot Act

— The United States government expands the scope of phone-tapping laws to thwart terrorism

— The United States sends forces to Afghanistan to topple the Taliban and expel Al-Qaeda leaders, including Osama bin Laden

— The Transportation Security Administration (TSA) is created to monitor travel

2002 — President George W. Bush creates the Department of Homeland Security

2003 — The United States sends forces to Iraq, which it accuses of sponsoring terrorism and having weapons of mass destruction, and ends the Hussein regime

2011 — Osama bin Laden is killed in a U.S. military raid in Pakistan

— The Iraq War comes to an end as the United States completes the withdrawal of its forces

2013 — The terrorist group known as the Islamic State of Iraq and Syria (ISIS) begins a campaign to retake Iraq

2014 — United States military forces return to Iraq to fight against ISIS

2015 — Congress passes the USA FREEDOM Act to renew the Patriot Act while also limiting the surveillance of American citizens

The War on Terror

This map shows countries in which the United States has conducted major operations related to the War on Terror since 2001, including the year of the beginning of each operation.

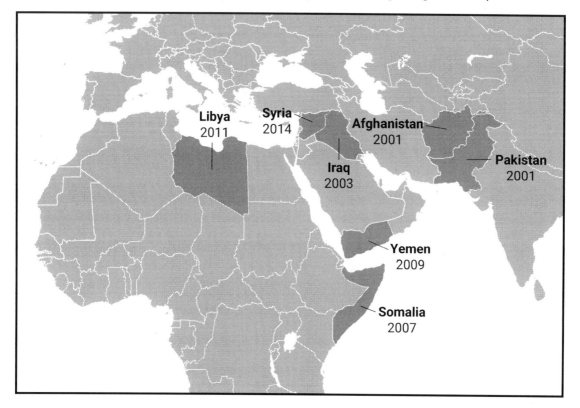

Question 19

Terrorist attacks against the United States had significant effects on U.S. foreign policy. Use the numbers in the flowchart to label the **four** relevant events below that show the effects of these attacks on U.S. foreign policy. Pay attention to chronological order.

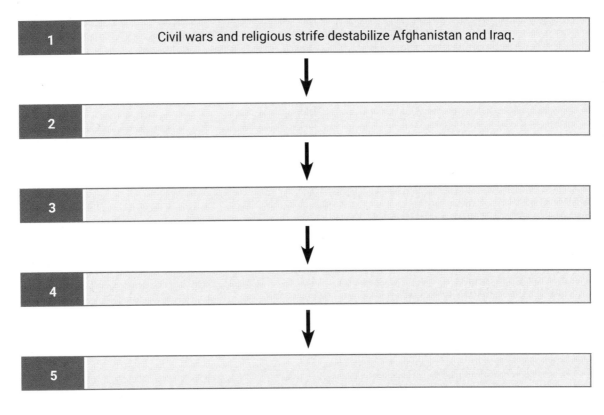

| 1 | Civil wars and religious strife destabilize Afghanistan and Iraq. |

| 2 | |

| 3 | |

| 4 | |

| 5 | |

_____ The United States military enacts a policy of non-involvement in the Middle East.

_____ Seeking to reduce instability in Iraq, the United States commits additional troops to its occupation of the region.

_____ The Taliban are deposed as leaders of Afghanistan by the United States and replaced with a new government.

_____ The United States invades Iraq, claiming its government possesses WMDs and are tied to Al-Qaeda.

_____ Taliban-linked terrorist group Al-Qaeda organizes a coordinated attack against the United States on September 11, 2001.

_____ Afghanistan and Iraq appeal to the United States for help.

The Passages Reboot

Instructions

Use what you know about finding the main idea of a passage to answer the question below.

Source 4

Excerpt from "Remarks on Decision Not to Seek Re-Election" (1968)

by President Lyndon Baines Johnson

This excerpt is from a speech given by President Lyndon B. Johnson to explain his decision not to run for president again in the 1968 election.

Tonight I want to speak to you of peace in Vietnam and Southeast Asia . . .

We shall accelerate the reequipment[1] of South Vietnam's armed forces—in order to meet the enemy's increased firepower. This will enable them progressively to undertake a larger share of combat operations against the Communist invaders . . .

Now let me give you my estimate of the chances for peace:

—the peace that will one day stop the bloodshed in South Vietnam,

—that will permit all the Vietnamese people to rebuild and develop their land,

—that will permit us to turn more fully to our own tasks here at home . . .

With America's sons in the fields far away, with America's future under challenge right here at home, with our hopes and the world's hopes for peace in the balance every day, I do not believe that I should devote an hour or a day of my time to any personal partisan[2] causes or to any duties other than the awesome duties of this office—the Presidency of your country.

Accordingly, I shall not seek, and I will not accept, the nomination of my party for another term as your President.

[1] **reequipment:** rearming

[2] **partisan:** political

Based on Source 4, which statement **best** explains why President Johnson chose not to run for another term?

A. Ending the Vietnam War was his only goal as president.

B. The Vietnam War was deeply unpopular with the American public.

C. There were too many political obstacles to ending the Vietnam War.

D. The Vietnam War prevented him from passing civil rights legislation.

Cross-References

Instructions

Refer to the sources and question below as your instructor leads the discussion. Write the numbers from the flowchart in front of the corresponding correct answer choices.

Special Mentions

Sometimes, the timelines will mention a specific event, era, or other key concept. But you don't have to rely on your memory. Use the titles of the other sources to find the one most likely to help you.

Source 2

Excerpt from "Address to the Nation About the Watergate Investigations" (1973)

by President Richard Nixon

This excerpt is from a speech given by President Richard Nixon to address the Watergate scandal.

In recent months, members of my Administration and officials of the Committee for the Re-Election of the President—including some of my closest friends and most trusted aides—have been charged with involvement in what has come to be known as the Watergate affair. These include charges of illegal activity during and preceding the 1972 Presidential election and charges that responsible officials participated in efforts to cover up that illegal activity . . .

Today, in one of the most difficult decisions of my Presidency, I accepted the resignations of two of my closest associates in the White House—Bob Haldeman, John Ehrlichman—two of the finest public servants it has been my privilege to know . . .

Whatever may appear to have been the case before, whatever improper activities may yet be discovered in connection with this whole sordid[1] affair, I want the American people, I want you to know beyond the shadow of a doubt that during my term as President, justice will be pursued fairly, fully, and impartially, no matter who is involved. This office is a sacred trust, and I am determined to be worthy of that trust.

Looking back at the history of this case, two questions arise:

How could it have happened?

Who is to blame? . . .

I will not place the blame on subordinates—on people whose zeal exceeded their judgment and who may have done wrong in a cause they deeply believed to be right.

In any organization, the man at the top must bear the responsibility. That responsibility, therefore, belongs here, in this office. I accept it. And I pledge to you tonight, from this office, that I will do everything in my power to ensure that the guilty are brought to justice and that such abuses are purged from our political processes in the years to come, long after I have left this office.

Some people, quite properly appalled at the abuses that occurred, will say that Watergate demonstrates the bankruptcy of the American political system. I believe precisely the opposite is true.

[1] **sordid:** scandalous

Source 3

Political Events of the 1960s and 1970s

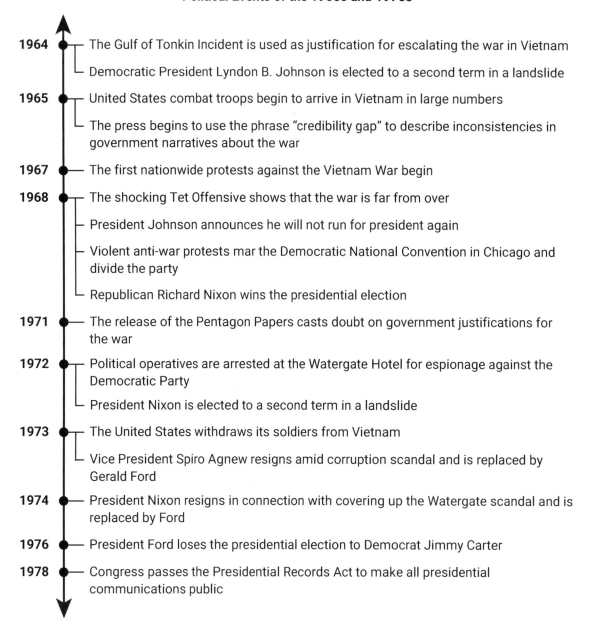

1964 — The Gulf of Tonkin Incident is used as justification for escalating the war in Vietnam

— Democratic President Lyndon B. Johnson is elected to a second term in a landslide

1965 — United States combat troops begin to arrive in Vietnam in large numbers

— The press begins to use the phrase "credibility gap" to describe inconsistencies in government narratives about the war

1967 — The first nationwide protests against the Vietnam War begin

1968 — The shocking Tet Offensive shows that the war is far from over

— President Johnson announces he will not run for president again

— Violent anti-war protests mar the Democratic National Convention in Chicago and divide the party

— Republican Richard Nixon wins the presidential election

1971 — The release of the Pentagon Papers casts doubt on government justifications for the war

1972 — Political operatives are arrested at the Watergate Hotel for espionage against the Democratic Party

— President Nixon is elected to a second term in a landslide

1973 — The United States withdraws its soldiers from Vietnam

— Vice President Spiro Agnew resigns amid corruption scandal and is replaced by Gerald Ford

1974 — President Nixon resigns in connection with covering up the Watergate scandal and is replaced by Ford

1976 — President Ford loses the presidential election to Democrat Jimmy Carter

1978 — Congress passes the Presidential Records Act to make all presidential communications public

Question 20

The Watergate scandal had many causes and was responsible for several effects on American society. Write C for Cause or E for Effect in front of the corresponding answer choices. Choose **two** causes and **two** effects of the Watergate scandal.

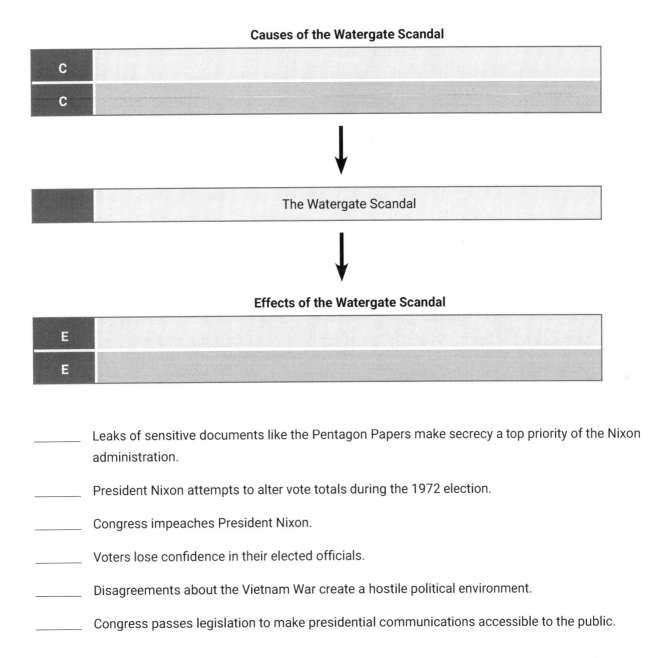

Causes of the Watergate Scandal

C	
C	

↓

The Watergate Scandal

↓

Effects of the Watergate Scandal

E	
E	

_____ Leaks of sensitive documents like the Pentagon Papers make secrecy a top priority of the Nixon administration.

_____ President Nixon attempts to alter vote totals during the 1972 election.

_____ Congress impeaches President Nixon.

_____ Voters lose confidence in their elected officials.

_____ Disagreements about the Vietnam War create a hostile political environment.

_____ Congress passes legislation to make presidential communications accessible to the public.

Under Construction

Instructions

Refer to Source 2 (page 78), Source 3 (page 80), and Source 4 (page 76), along with the information below. Use the space provided to create an outline for your answer to the writing prompt.

Content and Claims

When your constructed response answers are scored, the graders look at two main features:

→ Content – Did you get the answer right?

→ Claims – Does your evidence support your answer?

You get points for each, meaning that even if you get the answer wrong, giving evidence that supports your answer means still picking up some points.

> *Remember that your grade won't be affected by things like style, word choice, or sentence structure. Focus on getting the facts right and take a quick pass to pick out any typos or small mistakes once you're done typing.*

Question 21

Using the sources and your knowledge of U.S. history, explain how the political controversies of the 1960s and 1970s affected American society, providing examples of at least **two** differences between American society before the controversies and American society after the controversies.

ITEM SET WALKTHROUGH

Item Set Walkthrough Preview

Instructions

Complete the quiz. If time remains, check your answers.

What Is an Item Set?

On test day, you can expect to see these common features across all item sets:

- A shared event or era

- A mixture of four sources

- Questions that examine the sources in order

- A tech-enhanced question as the last question

> **Read and study the sources about the Great Depression and the New Deal. Then use the sources and your knowledge of U.S. history to answer the questions.**

This page intentionally left blank. Content resumes on the next page.

Item Set Walkthrough: Question 22

Instructions

Refer to the timeline and question below as your instructor leads the discussion.

Source 1

The Great Depression and the New Deal

1918 — The First World War ends, causing global food prices to sink and plunging American farmers into a cycle of debt

1929 — The stock market crashes, instantly wiping out billions of dollars of wealth

1930 — Dust storms known as the "Dust Bowl" begin to sweep across the Great Plains, eventually destroying millions of acres of crops

1932 — Franklin Delano Roosevelt (FDR) is elected president on a platform of instituting immediate economic relief and reform

1933 — FDR signs a flurry of New Deal laws during his famous "First 100 Days" in office, including the National Industrial Recovery Act to protect workers, the Agricultural Adjustment Act to stabilize food prices, and the Emergency Banking Act to insure bank deposits

1935 — The "Second New Deal" brings a second flurry of laws, creating agencies such as the National Labor Relations Board, which protects unions; the Social Security Administration, which provides stable retirement income; and the Resettlement Administration, which provides shelter for displaced families

1936 — FDR is elected to a second term in a landslide

1937 — The economy enters a brief recession after the government reduces spending and tightens money supply

1939 — The Second World War begins in Europe, shifting the United States into a fast-paced wartime economy and effectively ending the Great Depression

Question 22

Using Source 1, which statement describes a **main** cause of the Great Depression?

A. The government tried to control every aspect of the economy.

B. The economy was unable to respond to unpredictable events.

C. The economy failed to transition from agricultural to industrial production.

D. The government spent too many economic resources on war.

Item Set Walkthrough: Question 23

Instructions

Refer to the images and question below as your instructor leads the discussion.

Source 2

New Deal Posters

These posters were created during the Franklin D. Roosevelt administration.

What do you see in the CCC (Civilian Conservation Corps)? (c. 1940)

by U.S. Forestry Service

Source: Minnesota Historical Society

Federal Art Project Works Progress Administration (1936)

Source: Work Projects Administration Poster Collection, Library of Congress

Question 23

Using Source 2, which statements **best** describe ways in which the Civilian Conservation Corps (CCC) and the Works Progress Administration (WPA) helped the United States recover from the Great Depression?

Select the **two** correct answers.

A. The CCC provided training and careers in the military.

B. The WPA promoted membership in labor unions.

C. The CCC created rules to prevent future bank failures.

D. The WPA provided funding for important cultural projects.

E. The CCC helped the unemployed gain marketable skills.

F. The WPA offered loans to help small businesses recover.

Item Set Walkthrough: Question 24

Instructions

Refer to the passage and question below as your instructor leads the discussion.

Source 3

Excerpt from "Interview about dust storms in Oklahoma" (1940)

This excerpt includes the account of Flora Robertson, whose family survived the Dust Bowl, a series of dust storms that spread across the Great Plains during the 1930s.

We looked in the north and thought it was the Blue Norther[1] coming. Such a huge black cloud just looked like a smoke out of a train stack or something . . .

Our house was sealed but that dust come through somehow. Even those stucco[2] houses by all around the doors and the windows, the dust would be all piled so high and you just had to mop real good when it was over to get it out, you just couldn't get it out no other way . . .

Sometimes it would be a week before we would see the sun, it was just darkened. And sometimes the cloud would look black. Sometimes it would look red. It was pardoned on[3] which way the wind comes whether it was the red dirt was blowing over or the black dirt, or pardoned the way that the storm was coming. And we had cattle, we had cows that we gave, $60 and some $90 in dear old money. And we, uh, it killed a lamb, its name was Dottie. And we would cut their lungs open and it looked just like a mud pack or something. And it just really showed it was the mud.

[1] **Blue Norther:** a cold and stormy weather pattern marked by dark blue skies

[2] **stucco:** a strong building material with no gaps

[3] **pardoned on:** decided by

Dust Bowl Migration, 1935–1940

This map shows migration patterns that resulted from the Dust Bowl.

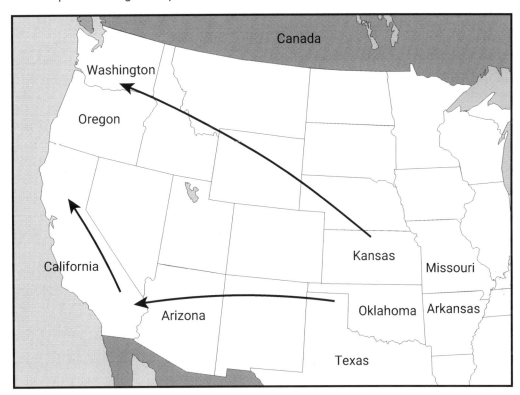

Question 24

Based on Sources 1 and 3, which statements **best** describe effects of the Dust Bowl?

Select the **two** correct answers.

A. Farmers throughout the Great Plains lost their livelihoods, forcing them to move.

B. Farmers withdrew their savings from Wall Street, causing the stock market to crash.

C. Franklin D. Roosevelt focused his relief efforts primarily on the agricultural sector of the economy.

D. Farmers sought to cultivate more fertile land east of the Mississippi River.

E. The Resettlement Administration created migrant camps in the western United States.

F. Discrimination against Chicano migrant workers became a national scandal.

Item Set Walkthrough: Question 25

Instructions

Refer to the passage and question below as your instructor leads the discussion.

Source 4

Excerpt from the State of the Union Address (January 4, 1935)

This excerpt is from an address to Congress delivered by President Franklin D. Roosevelt.

We have, however, a clear mandate[1] from the people, that Americans must forswear[2] that conception of the acquisition of wealth which, through excessive profits, creates undue private power over private affairs and, to our misfortune, over public affairs as well. In building toward this end[3] we do not destroy ambition, nor do we seek to divide our wealth into equal shares on stated occasions. We continue to recognize the greater ability of some to earn more than others. But we do assert that the ambition of the individual to obtain for him and his a proper security, a reasonable leisure[4], and a decent living throughout life, is an ambition to be preferred to the appetite for great wealth and great power.

I recall to your attention my message to the Congress last June in which I said: "among our objectives I place the security of the men, women and children of the nation first." That remains our first and continuing task; and in a very real sense every major legislative enactment[5] of this Congress should be a component part of it.

In defining immediate factors which enter into our quest, I have spoken to the Congress and the people of three great divisions:

1. The security of a livelihood through the better use of the national resources of the land in which we live.

2. The security against the major hazards and vicissitudes[6] of life.

3. The security of decent homes.

I am now ready to submit to the Congress a broad program designed ultimately to establish all three of these factors of security—a program which because of many lost years will take many future years to fulfill.

[1] **mandate:** command

[2] **forswear:** renounce

[3] **end:** goal

[4] **leisure:** enjoyment

[5] **legislative enactment:** passing of a law

[6] **vicissitudes:** unexpected occurrences

Question 25

Using Source 4, which statement **best** explains how President Franklin D. Roosevelt aimed to help the United States recover from the devastation caused by the Great Depression?

A. Roosevelt wanted to nationalize major corporations to stabilize the economy.

B. Roosevelt planned to stimulate economic growth by reducing regulations.

C. Roosevelt created a social safety net to protect Americans from economic hardship.

D. Roosevelt offered incentives for corporations to form strong monopolies.

Item Set Walkthrough: Question 26

Instructions

Refer back to Sources 1–4 and the tech-enhanced question below as your instructor leads the discussion.

Question 26

Drag and drop **two** correct causes of government intervention in the economy during the Great Depression and **two** correct effects of the Great Depression into the columns of the chart.

Causes of government intervention during the Great Depression	Effects of the Great Depression
_____	_____
_____	_____

1. The government discovers a communist conspiracy to influence the American economy.

2. The government significantly expands in size and employs vastly more people.

3. The government wants to bring immediate relief to families suffering from economic hardship.

4. The government implements extensive civil service reform.

5. The government increases regulations on banks with agencies such as the Federal Deposit Insurance Corporation.

6. The government loses the confidence of the American people.

7. High temperatures and dry conditions lead to thousands of acres of agricultural land drying up.

Item Set Walkthrough: Question 27

Instructions

Refer back to Sources 1–4 and the constructed response question below as your instructor leads the discussion.

Question 27

Using the sources and your knowledge of U.S. history, explain **two** different ways in which the New Deal contributed to bringing the United States out of the Great Depression.

I can use information from these sources to help me answer this question:

☐ Source 1

☐ Source 2

☐ Source 3

☐ Source 4

SECTION 7
MINI-TEST

Mini-Test

Instructions

Complete the mini-test. If time remains, check your answers.

Read and study the sources about robber barons and muckrakers in the late nineteenth and early twentieth centuries. Then use the sources and your knowledge of U.S. history to answer the questions.

Source 1

Major Industries in the United States

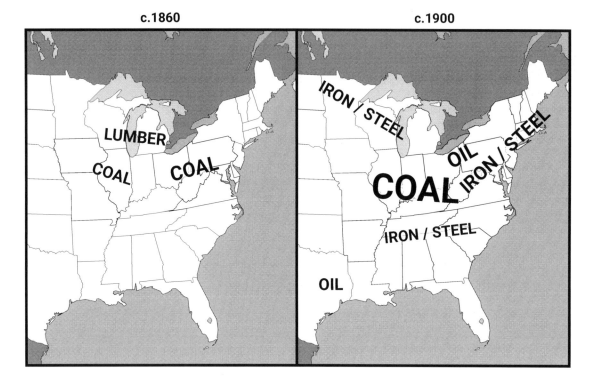

Question 1

Using Source 1, which statement **best** explains how the emergence of new industries affected business activity?

A. Technological developments gave rise to industries that concentrated in new economic centers.

B. The growth of new industries reduced the need for government regulation of monopolies.

C. Technological developments transferred power from business owners to employees and consumers.

D. The growth of new industries shifted the primary focus of business activity from cities to rural areas.

Source 2

The Popular Tendency To Rail at Wealth Is Not Entirely Justified (1897)

In this political cartoon from Puck, an angry crowd in the center, labeled "Chorus of the Poor Man, the Socialist, the Dissatisfied Laborer, the Populistic Farmer, the Demagogue,[1] the Chronic Idler,[2] and the Struggling Professional Man," shouts "Down with selfish, grasping Capital!"[3] Around the edges of the cartoon, starting at the top left, are scenes which show these people differently:

- "1) This is the Dissatisfied Laborer on Sunday, enjoying the benefaction[4] of the hated rich" at the "Museum of Art."

- "2) This is the Socialist at home, in one of the model, low-rent tenements, built by philanthropic[5] rich men."

- "3) These are a few things that the rich are doing for the Poor Man." This scene includes signs that say "Fresh air excursion[6] for poor mothers and children," "Free baths," "Free kindergarten for poor children," "Free milk for the poor," and "Free ice for the poor."

- "4) These are the sons of the Populistic Farmer and the Demagogue, and others of their kind, taking the educational advantages placed within their reach by the wealthy." This scene includes signs that say "Yalevard College: Founded and supported by legacies of wealthy citizens" and the names of other institutions "endowed"[7] by the wealthy.

- "5) This is the Chronic Idler, being nursed in sickness, through the benevolence[8] of 'grasping capital.'" This scene contains signs that say "free hospital" and "bed endowed" by various businessmen.

- "6) This is the Struggling Professional Man, using the endowments of wealth to carry on his calling" below a sign that reads, "Free library: The gift of Mr. Great Wealth."

[1]**demagogue:** a public speaker who appeals to the crowd

[2]**chronic idler:** someone who refuses to work

[3]**capital:** wealth

[4]**benefaction:** charity

[5]**philanthropic:** giving to charity

[6]**excursion:** cruise

[7]**endowed:** donated

[8]**benevolence:** generosity

Source: Samuel D. Ehrhart, 1897. Library of Congress

Question 2

Which statements would **most likely** have been supported by the cartoonist who created Source 2? Select **two** correct answers.

A. The wealthy took advantage of the poor.

B. Wealthy individuals provided essential services to society.

C. Laborers had little access to entertainment and culture.

D. Complaints about the greed of the wealthy were unfounded.

E. Wealth should be redistributed in a socialist economic system.

F. The president supported the interests of the wealthy over others.

Source 3

Excerpt from "Commercial Machiavellianism" (1906)
by Ida M. Tarbell

This magazine article was written by Ida M. Tarbell, a famous "muckraker" journalist and author.

Our modern captains of industry rarely lie or break the laws, bribe or practice cruelty, save for the sake of the end; that is they do not do these things for the sake of doing them as a Caligula or a Nero[1] would have done. They do them for the good of the business. Listen to one of our railroad officials who, recently on the stand, testified to granting a rebate.[2] "We knew it was illegal but it was the only way we could get our share of the business;" that is, the law is less important than the share of business.

In one great concern where for nearly forty years there is an unbroken record of lawbreaking and of spying and of hard dealings, the repeated explanation has been that it was for the good of the business. Not long ago a western senator of the United States was found guilty of stealing public lands. A former colleague openly justified him on the ground that by this robbery the land had been opened up[3] more quickly than it otherwise would have been. Wherever a case comes to the surface it is promptly justified as necessary to keep up the dividends,[4] expand trade, meet competition, get your share of the business, stimulate commerce. That is, in the minds of our commercial leaders the end justifies the means as much as it ever did in the mind of Cesare Borgia, the monks of the Spanish Inquisition, of Napoleon Bonaparte, or of Count Metternich.[5]

[1] **Caligula, Nero:** ancient Roman emperors who were famous for their cruelty

[2] **rebate:** a special discount given to a large company

[3] **opened up:** developed for business

[4] **dividends:** profits shared with investors

[5] **Cesare Borgia, the monks of the Spanish Inquisition, Napoleon Bonaparte, Count Metternich:** famous villains from European history

---

Question 3

Using Source 3, which reason **best** explains the goal of writers like Ida M. Tarbell?

A. to prevent wealthy industrialists from dominating the American economy

B. to convince politicians to develop more land for commercial use

C. to promote laws designed to limit economic competition

D. to stop the government from interfering in the American economy

Source 4

Timeline of Actions Taken Against Trusts in the United States

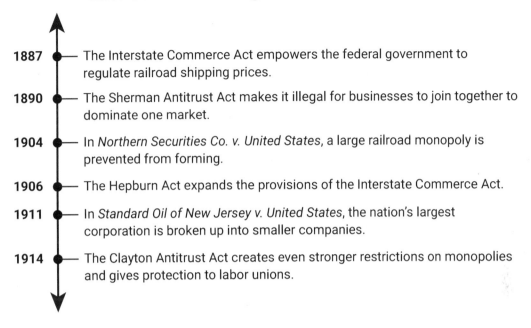

1887 — The Interstate Commerce Act empowers the federal government to regulate railroad shipping prices.

1890 — The Sherman Antitrust Act makes it illegal for businesses to join together to dominate one market.

1904 — In *Northern Securities Co. v. United States*, a large railroad monopoly is prevented from forming.

1906 — The Hepburn Act expands the provisions of the Interstate Commerce Act.

1911 — In *Standard Oil of New Jersey v. United States*, the nation's largest corporation is broken up into smaller companies.

1914 — The Clayton Antitrust Act creates even stronger restrictions on monopolies and gives protection to labor unions.

Question 4

Using Sources 3 and 4, which statement **best** describes a major economic problem faced by American consumers during the late nineteenth century?

A. Wages were low because of too much government regulation.

B. Prices were too high because of a lack of competition.

C. Small businesses were forced to close because of antitrust legislation.

D. Consumers lost access to certain goods because of railroad closures.

Question 5

The rise of American industrialization in the late nineteenth century had a significant impact on the development of the economy.

Draw lines from **four** correct events to indicate where in the flowchart they belong. Use chronological order from earliest to most recent to show the effects of industrialization on society.

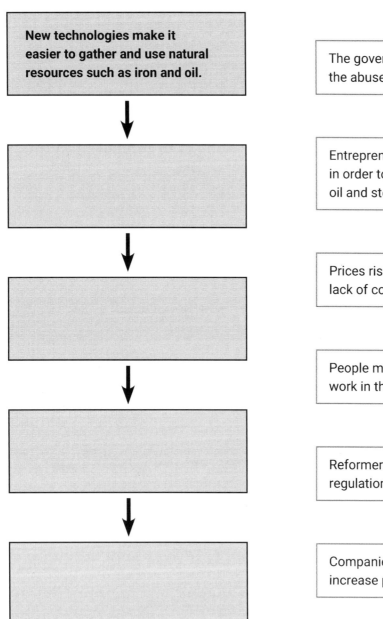

The government passes antitrust laws to curb the abuses of large corporations.

Entrepreneurs buy land and found companies in order to profit from new industries, such as oil and steel refinement.

Prices rise and wages shrink because of a lack of competition in major industries.

People move from cities to rural areas to find work in the oil and steel industries.

Reformers call for the government to reduce regulation of major industries.

Companies form monopolies in order to increase profits and market share.

Source 5

Excerpt from the War Powers Resolution

by the U.S. Department of Justice

Section 3 of the WPR calls for consultation "with Congress" "in every possible instance . . . before introducing United States Armed Forces" into hostile situations and "regularly" thereafter until hostilities cease or those forces have been removed.

Question 6

Which statement **best** explains why the public supported provisions such as those laid out in the War Powers Resolution of 1973?

A. The War Powers Resolution granted Congress exclusive authority in all international conflicts.

B. The War Powers Resolution led the government to prioritize foreign policy over domestic affairs.

C. The War Powers Resolution gave Congress authority to balance executive control over the military.

D. The War Powers Resolution increased the likelihood of U.S. involvement in international conflicts.

Source 6

Excerpt from "Starting the Real Business"

by Henry Ford

The new equipment and the whole progress of the company have always been financed out of earnings . . .

The original company and its equipment, as may be gathered, were not elaborate. We rented Strelow's carpenter shop on Mack Avenue. In making my designs . . . the entire car was made according to my designs . . . That would really be the most economical method of manufacturing. . . . The modern . . . method is to have each part made where it may best be made and then assemble the parts into a complete unit at the points of consumption. That is the method we are now following and expect to extend . . .

My associates were not convinced that it was possible to restrict our cars to a single model.

Question 7

Which quotation from "Starting the Real Business" by Henry Ford **best** represents the idea of specialization in the industrial age?

A. "The new equipment and the whole progress of the company have always been financed out of earnings."

B. "In making my designs . . . the entire car was made according to my designs."

C. "The modern . . . method is to have each part made where it may best be made . . ."

D. "My associates were not convinced that it was possible to restrict our cars to a single model."

Source 7

Major Events in Railroad Technology

Year	Event
1826	The first working railway is opened in Quincy, Massachusetts. Cargo is carried by horses.
1829	The first steam locomotive becomes operational in America.
1856	Englishman Henry Bessemer invents the Bessemer Steel Process.
1869	The first Transcontinental Railroad is completed in North America, connecting the Pacific coast with the Midwest.
1878	Gustavus Swift, along with Andrew Chase, creates the first refrigerated railcar.

Question 8

Which statement **best** explains how the technological innovations shown in the timeline made an impact on society?

A. American trade increased as the transport of goods became faster.

B. Employment rates decreased as technological advancements eliminated jobs.

C. Protests became more widespread with information traveling more easily.

D. Goods became more expensive because businesses had to invest in technology.

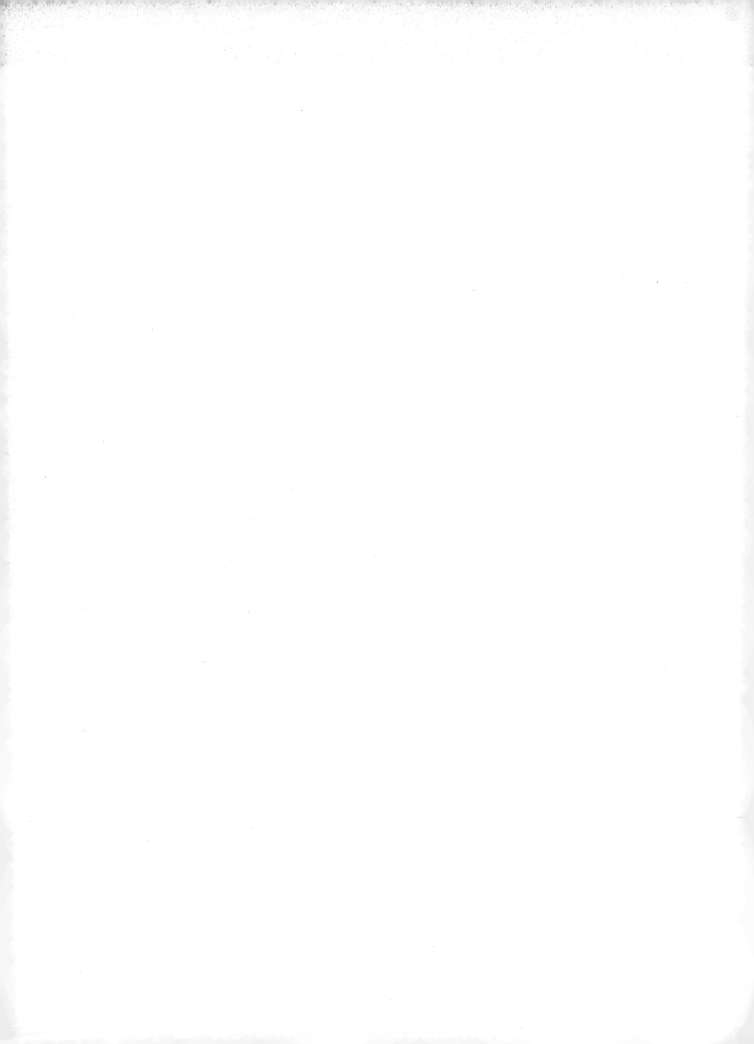

SECTION 8
CONCLUSION

Key Test-Taking Skills

Instructions

Refer to the following information as your instructor leads the discussion.

During the LEAP 2025 U.S. History test, remember:

- Never leave a question blank.

- Stay elimination focused.

- This is an open-book test. Use your sources!

- The timelines are invaluable for cause-and-effect or sequence questions.

- When it comes to the essay, evidence gets points.

Before the Test

Instructions

Refer to the following informattion as your instructor leads the discussion.

Before you take the LEAP 2025 U.S. History test, try to:

- Establish good sleeping habits.

- Eat breakfast.

- Minimize caffeine intake.

- Dress comfortably.

- Reduce distractions.

- Stay motivated!

CONTRIBUTORS

Director of Curriculum
Stephanie Constantino

Chief Product Officer
Oliver Pope

Director of Quality
Allison Eskind

Director of Design
Jeff Garrett

Curriculum Development Specialist
David Miller

Quality Control Coordinator
Conor Wallace

Interior Book Designer
Stephanie Pan

Lead Item Writer
Peter Franco

Project Manager
Luke Switzer

Cover and PPT Design
Nicole St. Pierre

ANSWER KEY

The Standalones

1 B

2 B, E

3 C

4 A

Test Run

5 C

6 B

7 D

Maps, Images, and Timelines

8 C, F

9 D

10 C, E

Test Run

11 D

12 B

The Passages

13	C
14	B
15	B

Maps, Images, and Timelines Reboot

Answer: **A**

Test Run

16	B
17	D

18 ==We had to put up with many insults and some frauds, as men would come in and claim parcels that did not belong to them==

==is one of the few opportunities that are open==

==He cannot practice any trade, and his opportunities to do business are limited to his own countrymen.==

==They are not allowed to bring wives here from China, and if they marry American women there is a great outcry==

Tech-Enhanced Questions

19

_____	The United States military enacts a policy of non-involvement in the Middle East.
4	Seeking to reduce instability in Iraq, the United States commits additional troops to its occupation of the region.
2	The Taliban are deposed as leaders of Afghanistan by the United States and replaced with a new government.
3	The United States invades Iraq, claiming its government possesses WMDs and are tied to Al-Qaeda.
1	Taliban-linked terrorist group Al-Qaeda organizes a coordinated attack against the United States on September 11, 2001.
_____	Afghanistan and Iraq appeal to the United States for help.

Tech-Enhanced Questions (cont.)

20   **C**   Leaks of sensitive documents like the Pentagon Papers make secrecy a top priority of the Nixon administration.

        President Nixon attempts to alter vote totals during the 1972 election.

        Congress impeaches President Nixon.

  E   Voters lose confidence in their elected officials.

  C   Disagreements about the Vietnam War create a hostile political environment.

  E   Congress passes legislation to make presidential communications accessible to the public.

The Passages Reboot

Answer: **B**

Under Construction

21 Correct answer:
Include at least two of the following:

- **Widespread distrust in public officials**
- **Greater partisanship**
- **Intense media coverage of politicians**
- **Loss of presidential power to Congress and the people**
- **Greater controversy surrounding military actions of the government**
- **Frequent impeachments**

Item Set Walkthrough

22 B

23 D, E

24 A, E

25 C

26

Causes of government intervention during the Great Depression	Effects of the Great Depression
3. The government wants to bring immediate relief to families suffering from economic hardship.	2. The government significantly expands in size and employs vastly more people.
7. High temperatures and dry conditions lead to thousands of acres of agricultural land drying up.	5. The government increases regulations on banks with programs such as the Federal Deposit Insurance Corporation.

27 Correct answer:

A constructed response essay that explains how The New Deal accomplished at least two of the following:

- Brought immediate financial relief to suffering families
- Created a social safety net that prevented additional suffering
- Reformed the economy to prevent dangerous fluctuations from occurring again
- Expanded government power to take decisive action
- Created and promoted public works, including art and music
- Provided jobs and training to put Americans back to work

Mini-Test

1 A

2 B, D

3 A

4 B

5

> New technologies make it easier to gather and use natural resources such as iron and oil.

> Entrepreneurs buy land and found companies in order to profit from new industries, such as oil and steel refinement.

> Companies form monopolies in order to increase profits and market share.

> Prices rise and wages shrink because of a lack of competition in major industries.

> The government passes antitrust laws to curb the abuses of large corporations.

Mini-Test (cont.)

6 C

7 C

8 A

Made in the USA
Columbia, SC
11 April 2023